DANIEL BOONE.

THE LIFE AND ADVENTURES OF DANIEL BOONE,

THE FIRST SETTLER OF KENTUCKY,

INTERSPERSED WITH INCIDENTS IN THE

EARLY ANNALS OF THE COUNTRY.

BY TIMOTHY FLINT.

NEW EDITION

To which is added an account of Captain Estill's Defeat.

CINCINNATI:
PUBLISHED BY U. P. JAMES,
NO. 167 WALNUT STREET.
1868.

Entered according to Act of Congress, in the year 1857,

By U. P. JAMES,

in the Clerk's Office of the District Court of the United States, for the Southern District of Ohio.

THE ENGRAVINGS

on pages 2, 22, 42, 54, 66, 70, 76, 95, 120, and 146 were made for the original edition, and, therefore, are retained in this.

CONTENTS.

CHAPTER I.

Birth of Daniel Boone—His early propensities—His pranks at school—His first hunting expedition—And his encounter with a panther. Removal of the family to North Carolina—Boone becomes a hunter—Description of fire hunting, in which he was near committing a sad mistake—Its fortunate result—and his marriage.

CHAPTER II.

Boone removes to the head waters of the Yadkin river—He meets with Finley, who had crossed the mountains into Tennessee—They agree to explore the wilderness west of the Alleghanies together.

CHAPTER III.

Boone, with Finley and others, start on their exploring expedition—Boone kills a panther in the night—Their progress over the mountains—They descend into the great valley—Description of the new country—Herds of buffaloes—Their wanderings in the wilderness.

CHAPTER IV.

The exploring party divide into different routes—Boone and Stewart taken prisoners by the Indians, and their escape—Boone meets with his elder brother and another white man in the woods—Stewart killed by the Indians, and the companion of the elder Boone destroyed by wolves—The elder brother returns to North Carolina, leaving Boone alone in the wilderness.

CHAPTER V.

Boone is pursued by the Indians, and eludes their pursuit—He encounters and kills a bear—The return of his brother with ammunition—They explore the country—Boone kills a panther on the back of a buffalo—They return to North Carolina.

CHAPTER VI.

Boone starts with his family to Kentucky—Their return to Clinch river—He conducts a party of surveyors to the Falls of Ohio—He helps build Boonesborough, and removes his family to the fort—His daughter and two of Col. Calloway's daughters taken prisoners by the Indians—They pursue the Indians and rescue the captives.

CHAPTER VII.

Settlement of Harrodsburgh—Indian mode of besieging and warfare—Fortitude and privation of the Pioneers—The Indians attack Harrodsburgh and Boonesborough—Description of a Station—Attack of Bryant's Station.

CONTENTS.

CHAPTER VIII.

Boone being attacked by two Indians near the Blue Licks, kills them both—Is afterwards taken prisoner and marched to Old Chillicothe—Is adopted by the Indians—Indian ceremonies.

CHAPTER IX.

Boone becomes a favorite among the Indians—Anecdotes relating to his captivity—Their mode of tormenting and burning prisoners—Their fortitude under the infliction of torture—Concerted attack on Boonesborough—Boone escapes.

CHAPTER X.

Six hundred Indians attack Boonesborough—Boone and Captain Smith go out to treat with the enemy under a flag of truce, and are extricated from a treacherous attempt to detain them as prisoners—Defence of the fort—The Indians defeated—Boone goes to North Carolina to bring back his family.

CHAPTER XI.

A sketch of the character and adventures of several other pioneers—Harrod, Kenton, Logan, Ray, McAffee, and others.

CHAPTER XII.

Boone's brother killed, and Boone himself narrowly escapes from the Indians—Assault upon Ashton's station—and upon the station near Shelbyville—Attack upon McAffee's station.

CHAPTER XIII.

Disastrous battle near the Blue Licks—General Clarke's expedition against the Miami towns—Massacre of McClure's family—The horrors of Indian assaults throughout the settlements—General Harmar's expedition—Defeat of General St. Clair—Gen. Wayne's victory, and a final peace with the Indians.

CHAPTER XIV.

Rejoicings on account of the peace—Boone indulges his propensity for hunting—Kentucky increases in population—Some account of their conflicting land titles—Progress of civil improvement destroying the range of the hunter—Litigation of land titles—Boone loses his lands—Removes from Kentucky to the Kanawha—Leaves the Kanawha and goes to Missouri, where he is appointed Commandant.

CHAPTER XV.

Anecdotes of Colonel Boone, related by Mr. Audubon—A remarkable instance of memory.

CHAPTER XVI.

Progress of improvement in Missouri—Old age of Boone—Death of his wife—He goes to reside with his son—His death—His personal appearance and character.

PREFACE.

Our eastern brethren have entered heartily into the pious duty of bringing to remembrance the character and deeds of their forefathers. Shall we of the west allow the names of those great men, who won for us, from the forest, the savages, and wild beasts, our fair domain of fertile fields and beautiful rivers, to fade into oblivion? They who have hearts to admire nobility imparted by nature's great seal—fearlessness, strength, energy, sagacity, generous forgetfulness of self, the delineation of scenes of terror, and the relation of deeds of daring, will not fail to be interested in a sketch of the life of the pioneer and hunter of Kentucky, Daniel Boone. Contemplated in any light, we shall find him in his way and walk, a man as truly great as Penn, Marion, and Franklin, in theirs. True, he was not learned in the lore of books, or trained in the etiquette of cities. But he possessed a knowledge far more important in the sphere which Providence called him to fill. He felt, too, the conscious dignity of self-respect, and would have been seen as erect, firm, and unembarrassed amid the pomp and splendor of the proudest court in Christendom, as in the shade of his own wilderness. Where nature in her own ineffaceable characters has marked superiority, she looks down upon the tiny and elaborate acquirements of art, and in all positions and in all time entitles her favorites to the involuntary homage of their fellow-men. They are the selected pilots in storms, the leaders in battles, and the pioneers in the colonization of new countries.

Such a man was Daniel Boone, and wonderfully was he endowed by Providence for the part which he was called to act. Far be it from us to undervalue the advantages of education: It can do every thing but assume the prerogative of Providence. God has reserved for himself the attribute of creating. Distinguished excellence has never been attained, unless where nature and education, native endowment and circumstances, have concurred. This wonderful man received his commission for his achievements and his peculiar walk from the sign manual of nature. He was formed to be a woodsman, and the adventurous precursor in the first settlement of Kentucky. His home was in the woods, where others were bewildered and lost. It is a mysterious spectacle to see a man possessed of such an astonishing power of being perfectly familiar with his route and his resources in the depths of the untrodden wilderness, where others could as little divine their way, and what was to be done, as mariners on mid-ocean, without chart or compass, sun, moon, or stars. But that nature has bestowed these endowments upon some men and denied them to others, is as certain as that she has given to some animals instincts of one kind, fitting them for peculiar modes of life, which are denied to others, perhaps as strangely endowed in another way.

The following pages aim to present a faithful picture of this singular man, in his wanderings, captivities, and escapes. If the effort be successful, we have no fear that the attention of the reader will wander. There is a charm in such recitals, which lays its spell upon all. The grave and gay, the simple and the learned, the young and gray-haired alike yield to its influence.

We wish to present him in his strong incipient manifestations of the development of his peculiar character in boyhood. We then see him on foot and alone, with no companion but his dog, and no friend but his rifle, making his way over trackless and unnamed mountains, and immeasurable forests, until he explores the flowering wilderness of Kentucky. Already familiar, by his own peculiar intuition, with the Indian character, we see him casting his keen and searching glance around, as the ancient woods rung with the first strokes of his axe, and pausing from time to time to see if the echoes have startled the red men, or the wild beasts from their lair. We trace him through all the succeeding explorations of the Bloody Ground, and of Tennessee, until so many immigrants have followed in his steps, that he finds his privacy too strongly pressed upon; until he finds the buts and bounds of legal tenures restraining his free thoughts, and impelling him to the distant and unsettled shores of the Missouri, to seek range and solitude anew. We see him there, his eyes beginning to grow dim with the influence of seventy winters—as he can no longer take the unerring aim of his rifle—casting wistful looks in the direction of the Rocky Mountains and the western sea; and sadly reminded that man has but one short life, in which to wander.

No book can be imagined more interesting than would have been the personal narrative of such a man, written by himself. What a new pattern of the heart he might have presented! But, unfortunately, he does not seem to have dreamed of the chance that his adventures would go down to posterity in the form of recorded biography. We suspect that he rather eschewed books, parchment deeds, and clerkly contrivances, as forms of evil; and held the dead letter of little consequence. His associates were as little likely to preserve any records, but those of memory, of the daily incidents and exploits, which indicate character and assume high interest, when they relate to a person like the subject of this narrative. These hunters, unerring in their aim to prostrate the buffalo on his plain, or to bring down the geese and swans from the clouds, thought little of any other use of the gray goose quill, than its market value.

Had it been otherwise, and had these men themselves furnished the materials of this narrative, we have no fear that it would go down to futurity, a more enduring monument to these pioneers and hunters, than the granite columns reared by our eastern brethren, amidst assembled thousands, with magnificent array, and oratory, and songs, to the memory of their forefathers. Ours would be the record of human nature speaking to human nature in simplicity and truth, in a language always impressive, and always understood. Their pictures of their own felt sufficiency to themselves, under the pressure of exposure and want; of danger, wounds, and captivity; of reciprocal kindness, warm from the heart; of noble forgetfulness of self, unshrinking firmness, calm endurance, and reckless bravery, would be sure to move in the hearts of their readers strings which never fail to vibrate to the touch.

But these inestimable data are wanting. Our materials are comparatively few; and we have been often obliged to balance between doubtful authorities, notwithstanding the most rigorous scrutiny of newspapers and pamphlets, whose yellow and dingy pages gave out a cloud of dust at every movement, and the equally rigid examination of clean modern books and periodicals.

LIFE OF DANIEL BOONE.

CHAPTER I.

Birth of Daniel Boone—His early propensities—His pranks at school—His first hunting expedition—And his encounter with a panther. Removed of the family to North Carolina—Boone becomes a hunter—Description of fire hunting, in which he was near committing a sad mistake—Its fortunate result—and his marriage.

DIFFERENT authorities assign a different birth place to DANIEL BOONE. One affirms that he was born in Maryland, another in North Carolina, another in Virginia, and still another during the transit of his parents across the Atlantic. But they are all equally in error. He was born in the year 1746, in Bucks county, Pennsylvania, near Bristol, on the right bank of the Delaware, about twenty miles from Philadelphia. His father removed, when he was three years old, to the vicinity of Reading, on the head waters of the Schuylkill. From thence, when his son was thirteen years old, he migrated to North Carolina, and settled in one of the valleys of South Yadkin.

The remotest of his ancestors, of whom there is any recorded notice, is Joshua Boone, an English

Catholic. He crossed the Atlantic to the shores of the Chesapeake Bay, with those who planted the first germ of the colony of Maryland. A leading motive to emigration with most of these colonists, was to avoid that persecution on account of their religion, which however pleasant to inflict, they found it uncomfortable to endure. Whether this gentleman emigrated from this inducement, as has been asserted, or not, it is neither possible, nor, as we deem, important to settle; for we cannot find, that religious motives had any direct influence in shaping the character and fortunes of the hero of the woods. Those who love to note the formation of character, and believe in the hereditary transmission of peculiar qualities, naturally investigate the peculiarities of parents, to see if they can find there the origin of those of the children. Many—and we are of the number—consider transmitted endowment as the most important link in the chain of circumstances, with which character is surrounded. The most splendid endowments in innumerable instances, have never been brought to light, in defect of circumstances to call them forth. The ancestors of Boone were not placed in positions to prove, whether he did or did not receive his peculiar aptitudes a legacy from his parents, or a direct gift from nature. He presents himself to us as a new man, the author and artificer of his own fortunes, and showing from the beginning rudiments of character, of which history has recorded no trace in his ancestors. The promise of the future hunter appeared in his earliest boyhood. He waged a war of extermination, as soon as he could poise a gun, with squirrels, racoons, and wild cats, at that time exceedingly annoying to the fields and barn-yards of the back settlers.

No scholar ever displayed more decided pre-eminence in any branch of learning, than he did above the boys of his years, in adroitness and success in this species of hunting. This is the only distinct and peculiar trait of character recorded of his early years. The only transmitted fact of his early training is presented in the following anecdote.

In that section of the frontier settlement to which Boone had removed, where unhewn log cabins, and hewn log houses, were interspersed among the burnt stumps, surrounded by a potato patch and cornfield, as the traveller pursued his cow-path through the deep forest, there was an intersection, or more properly concentration of wagon tracks, called the "Cross Roads,"—a name which still designates a hundred frontier positions of a post office, blacksmith's shop, and tavern. In the central point of this metropolis stood a large log building, before which a sign creaked in the wind, conspicuously lettered "Store and Tavern."

To this point, on the early part of a warm spring morning, a pedestrian stranger was seen approaching in the path leading from the east. One hand was armed with a walking stick, and the other carried a small bundle inclosed in a handkerchief. His aspect was of a man, whose whole fortunes were in his walking stick and bundle. He was observed to eye the swinging sign with a keen recognition, inspiring such courage as the mariner feels on entering the desired haven.

His dialect betrayed the stranger to be a native of Ireland. He sat down on the *stoup*, and asked in his own peculiar mode of speech, for cold water. A supply from the spring was readily handed him in a gourd. But with an arch pause between remonstrance and laughter, he added, that he thought cold water in a warm climate injurious to the stomach and begged that the element might be qualified with a little whisky.

The whisky was handed him, and the usual conversation ensued, during which the stranger inquired if a school-master was wanted in the settlement—or, as he was pleased to phrase it, a professor in the higher branches of learning? It is inferred that the father of Boone was a person of distinction in the settlement, for to him did the master of the "Store and Tavern" direct the stranger of the staff and bundle for information.

The direction of the landlord to enable him to find the house of Mr. Boone, was a true specimen of similar directions in the frontier settlements of the present; and they have often puzzled clearer heads than that of the Irish school-master.

"Step this way," said he, "and I will direct you there, so that you cannot mistake your way. Turn down that right hand road, and keep on it till you cross the dry branch—then turn to your left, and go up a hill—then take a lane to your right, which will bring you to an open field—pass this, and you will come to a path with three forks—take the middle fork, and it will lead you through the woods in sight of Mr. Boone's plantation."

The Irishman lost his way, invoked the saints, and cursed his director for his medley of directions many a time, before he stumbled at length on Mr. Boone's house. He was invited to sit down and dine, in the simple backwoods phrase, which is still the passport to the most ample hospitality.

After dinner, the school-master made known his vocation, and his desire to find employment. To obtain a qualified school-master in those days, and in such a place, was no easy business. This scarcity of supply precluded close investigation of fitness. In a word, the Irishman was authorized to enter upon the office of school-master of the settlement. We have been thus particular in this description, because it was the way in which most teachers were then employed.

It will not be amiss to describe the school-house; for it stood as a sample of thousands of west country school-houses of the present day. It was of logs, after the usual fashion of the time and place. In dimension, it was spacious and convenient. The chimney was peculiarly ample, occupying one entire side of the whole building, which was an exact square. Of course, a log could be "snaked" to the fire-place as long as the building, and a file of boys thirty feet in length, could all stand in front of the fire on a footing of the most democratic equality. Sections of logs cut out here and there, admitted light and air instead of windows. The surrounding forest furnished ample supplies of fuel. A spring at hand, furnished with various gourds, quenched the frequent thirst of the pupils. A ponderous puncheon door, swinging on substantial wooden hinges, and shutting with a wooden latch, completed the appendages of this primeval seminary.

To this central point might be seen wending from the woods, in every direction of the compass, flaxen-headed boys and girls, clad in homespun, brushing away the early dews, as they hied to the place, where the Hibernian, clothed in his brief authority, sometimes perpetrated applications of birch without rhyme or reason; but much oftener allowed his authority to be trampled upon, according as the severe or loving humor prevailed. This vacillating administration was calculated for any result, rather than securing the affectionate respect of the children. Scarcely the first quarter had elapsed, before materials for revolt had germinated under the very throne of the school-master.

Young Boone, at this time, had reached the second stage of teaching the young idea how to shoot. His satchel already held paper marked with those mysterious hieroglyphics, vulgarly called *pot-hooks*, intended to be gradually transformed to those clerkly characters, which are called hand-writing.

The master's throne was a block of a huge tree, and could not be said, in any sense, to be a cushion of down. Of course, by the time he had heard the first lessons of the morning, the master was accustomed to let loose his noisy subjects, to wanton and bound on the grass, while he took a turn abroad to refresh himself from his wearying duties. While he was thus unbending his mind, the observant urchins had remarked, that he always directed his walk to a deep grove not far distant. They had, possibly, divined that the unequal tempers of his mind, and his rapid transitions from good nature to tyrannical moroseness, and the reverse, were connected with these promenades. The curiosity of young Boone had been partially excited. An opportunity soon offered to gratify it.

Having one day received the accustomed permission to retire a few minutes from school, the darting of a squirrel across a fallen tree, as he went abroad, awakened his ruling passion. He sprang after the nimble animal, until he found himself at the very spot, where he had observed his school-master to pause in his promenades. His attention was arrested by observing a kind of opening under a little arbor, thickly covered with a mat of vines. Thinking, perhaps, that it was the retreat of some animal, he thrust in his hand, and to his surprise drew forth a glass bottle, partly full of whisky. The enigma of his master's walks and inequalities of temper stood immediately deciphered. After the reflection of a moment, he carefully replaced the bottle in its position, and returned to his place in school. In the evening he communicated his discovery and the result of his meditations to the larger boys of the school on their way home. They were ripe for revolt, and the issue of their caucus follows:

They were sufficiently acquainted with fever and ague, to have experimented the nature of tartar emetic. They procured a bottle exactly like the

2

master's, filled with whisky, in which a copious quantity of emetic had been dissolved. Early in the morning, they removed the school-master's bottle, and replaced it by theirs, and hurried back to their places, panting with restrained curiosity, and a desire to see what results would come from their medical mixture.

The accustomed hour for intermission came. The master took his usual promenade, and the children hastened back with uncommon eagerness to resume their seats and their lessons. The countenance of the master alternately red and pale, gave portent of an approaching storm.

"Recite your grammar lesson," said he, in a growling tone, to one of the older boys.

"How many parts of speech are there?"

"Seven, sir," timidly answered the boy.

"Seven, you numscull! is that the way you get your lesson?" Forthwith descended a shower of blows on his devoted head.

"On what continent is Ireland?" said he, turning from him in wrath to another boy. The boy saw the shower pre-determined to fall, and the medicine giving evident signs of having taken effect. Before he could answer, "I reckon on the continent of England," he was gathering an ample tithe of drubbing.

"Come and recite your lesson in arithmetic?" said he to Boone, in a voice of thunder. The usually rubicund face of the Irishman was by this time a deadly pale. Slate in hand, the docile lad presented himself before his master.

"Take six from nine,and what remains ?"

"Three, sir."

"True. That will answer for whole numbers, now for your fractions. Take three-quarters from an integer, and what remains?"

"The whole."

"You blockhead! you numscull!" exclaimed the master, as the strokes fell like a hail shower; "let me hear you demonstrate that."

"If I subtract one bottle of whisky, and replace it with one in which I have mixed an emetic, will not the whole remain, if nobody drinks it?"

By this time the medicine was taking fearful effect. The united acclamations and shouts of the children, and the discovery of the compounder of his medicament, in no degree tended to soothe the infuriated master. Young Boone, having paid for his sport by an ample drubbing, seized the opportune moment, floored his master, already weak and dizzy, sprang from the door, and made for the woods. The adventure was soon blazoned. A consultation of the patrons of the school was held. Though young Boone was reprimanded, the master was dismissed.

This is all the certain information we possess, touching the training of young Boone, in the lore of books and schools. Though he never afterwards could be brought back to the restraint of the walls of a school, it is well known, that in some way, in after life, he possessed himself of the rudiments of a common education. His love for hunting and the woods now became an absorbing passion. He possessed a dog and a fowling piece, and with these he would range whole days alone through the woods, often with no other apparent object, than the simple pleasure of these lonely wanderings.

One morning he was observed as usual, to throw the band, that suspended his shot bag, over one shoulder, and his gun over the other, and go forth accompanied by his dog. Night came, but to the astonishment and alarm of his parents, the boy, as yet scarcely turned of fourteen, came not. Another day and another night came, and passed, and still he returned not. The nearest neighbors, sympathizing with the distressed parents, who considered him lost, turned out, to aid in searching for him. After a long and weary search, at a distance of a league from any plantation, a smoke was seen arising from a temporary hovel of sods and branches, in which the astonished father found his child, apparently most comfortably established is his new experiment of house-keeping. Numerous skins of wild animals were stretched upon his cabin, as trophies of his hunting prowess. Ample fragments of their flesh were either roasting or preparing for cookery. It may be supposed, that such a lad would be the theme of wonder and astonishment to the other boys of his age.

At this early period, he hesitated not to hunt wolves, and even bears and panthers. His exploits of this kind were the theme of general interest in the vicinity. Many of them are recorded. But we pass over most of them, in our desire to hasten to the exploits of his maturer years. We select a single one of the most unquestionable character, as a sample for the rest.

In company with some of his young companions he undertook a hunting excursion, at a considerable distance from the settlements. Near night-fall, the group of young Nimrods were alarmed with a sharp cry from the thick woods. A panther! whispered the affrighted lads, in accents scarcely above their breath, through fear, that their voice would betray them. The scream of this animal is harsh, and grating, and one of the most truly formidable of forest sounds.

The animal, when pressed, does not shrink from encountering a man, and often kills him, unless he is fearless and adroit in his defence. All the companions of young Boone fled from the vicinity, as fast as possible. Not so the subject of our narrative. He coolly surveyed the animal, that in turn eyed him, as the cat does a mouse, when preparing to spring upon it. Levelling his rifle, and taking deliberate aim, he lodged the bullet in the heart of the fearful animal, at the very moment it was in the act to spring upon him. It was a striking instance of that peculiar self-possession, which constituted the most striking trait in his character in after life.

Observing these early propensities for the life of a hunter in his son, and land having become dear and game scarce in the neighborhood where he lived Boone's father formed the design of removing to remote forests, not yet disturbed by the sound of the axe, or broken by frequent clearings; and having heard a good account of the country bordering upon

the Yadkin river, in North Carolina, he resolved to remove thither. This river, which is a stream of considerable size, has its source among the mountains in the north-east part of North Carolina, and pursues a beautiful meandering course through that state until it enters South Carolina. After watering the eastern section of the latter state, it reaches the ocean a few miles above the mouth of the Santee.

Having sold his plantation, on a fine April morning he set forth for the land of promise—wife, children, servants, flocks, and herds, forming a patriarchal caravan through the wilderness. No procession bound to the holy cities of Mecca or Jerusalem, was ever more joyful; for to them the forest was an asylum. Overhung by the bright blue sky, enveloped in verdant forests full of game, nought cared they for the absence of houses with their locks and latches. Their nocturnal caravansary was a clear cool spring; their bed the fresh turf. Deer and turkeys furnished their viands—hunger the richest sauces of cookery; and fatigue and untroubled spirits a repose unbroken by dreams. Such were the primitive migrations of the early settlers of our country. We love to meditate on them, for we have shared them. We have fed from this table in the wilderness. We have shared this mirth. We have heard the tinkle of the bells of the flocks and herds grazing among the trees. We have seen the moon rise and the stars twinkle upon this forest scene; and the remembrance has more than once marred the pleasure of journeyings in the midst of civilization and the refinements of luxury.

The frontier country in which the family settled was as yet an unbroken forest; and being at no great distance from the eastern slope of the Alleghanies, in the valleys of which game was abundant, it afforded fine range both for pasture and hunting. These forests had, moreover, the charm of novelty; and the game had not yet learned to fear the rifles of the new settlers. It need hardly be added that the spirits of young Boone exulted in this new hunter's paradise. The father and the other sons settled down quietly to the severe labor of making a farm, assigning to Daniel the occupation of his rifle, as aware that it was the only one he could be induced to follow; and probably from the experience, that in this way he could contribute more effectually to the establishment, than either of them in the pursuits of husbandry.

An extensive farm was soon opened. The table was always amply supplied with venison, and was the seat of ample and unostentatious hospitality. The peltries of the young hunter yielded all the money which such an establishment required, and the interval between this removal and the coming of age of young Boone, was one of health, plenty, and privacy.

But meanwhile this settlement began to experience the pressure of that evil which Boone always considered the greatest annoyance of life. The report of this family's prosperity had gone abroad. The young hunter's fame in his new position, attracted other immigrants to come and fix themselves in the vicinity. The smoke of new cabins and clearings went up to the sky. The baying of other dogs, and the crash of distant falling trees began to be heard; and painful presentiments already filled the bosom of young Boone, that this abode would shortly be more pressed upon than that he had left. He was compelled, however, to admit, that if such an order of things brings disadvantages, it has also its benefits.

A thriving farmer, by the name of Bryan, had settled at no great distance from Mr. Boone, by whose establishment the young hunter, now at the period of life when other thoughts than those of the chase of wild game are sometimes apt to cross the mind, was accustomed to pass.

This farmer had chosen a most beautiful spot for his residence. The farm occupied a space of some hundred acres on a gentle eminence, crested with yellow poplars and laurels. Around it rolled a mountain stream. So beautiful was the position and so many its advantages, that young Boone used often to pause in admiration, on his way to the deeper woods beyond the verge of human habitation. Who can say that the same dreamy thoughts that inspired the pen of the eloquent Rousseau, did not occupy the mind of the young hunter as he passed this rural abode? We hope we shall not be suspected of a wish to offer a tale of romance, as we relate, how the mighty hunter of wild beasts and men was himself subdued, and that by the most timid and gentle of beings. We put down the facts as we find them recorded, and our conscience is quieted, by finding them perfectly natural to the time, place, and circumstances.

Young Boone was one night engaged in a fire hunt, with a young friend. Their course led them to the deeply timbered bottom that skirted the stream which wound round this pleasant plantation. That the reader may have an idea what sort of a pursuit it was that young Boone was engaged in, during an event so decisive of his future fortunes, we present a brief sketch of a night *fire* hunt. Two persons are indispensable to it. The horseman that precedes, bears on his shoulder what is called a *fire pan*, full of blazing pine knots, which casts a bright and flickering glare far through the forest. The second follows at some distance, with his rifle prepared for action. No spectacle is more impressive than this of pairs of hunters, thus kindling the forest into a glare. The deer, reposing quietly in his thicket, is awakened by the approaching cavalcade, and instead of flying from the portentous brilliance, remains stupidly gazing upon it, as if charmed to the spot. The animal is betrayed to its doom by the gleaming of its fixed and innocent eyes. This cruel mode of securing a fatal shot, is called in hunter's phrase, *shining the eyes*.

The two young men reached a corner of the farmer's field at an early hour in the evening. Young Boone gave the customary signal to his mounted companion preceding him, to stop, an indication that he had *shined the eyes* of a deer. Boone dismounted, and fastened his horse to a tree. Ascertaining that his rifle was in order, he advanced cautiously behind a covert of bushes, to reach the right distance for a shot. The deer is remarkable for the beauty of its eyes when thus *shined.* The mild brilliance of the two orbs was distinctly visible. Whether warned by a presentiment, or arrested by a palpitation, and strange feelings within, at noting a new expression in the blue and dewy lights that gleamed to his heart, we say not. But the unerring rifle fell, and a rustling told him that the game had fled. Something whispered him it was not a *deer;* and yet the fleet step, as the game bounded away, might easily be mistaken for that of the light-footed animal. A second thought impelled him to pursue the rapidly retreating game; and he sprang away in the direction of the sound, leaving his companion to occupy himself as he might. The fugitive had the advantage of a considerable advance of him, and apparently a better knowledge of the localities of the place. But the hunter was perfect in all his field exercises, and scarcely less fleet footed than a deer; and he gained rapidly on the object of his pursuit, which advanced a little distance parallel with the field-fence, and then, as if endowed with the utmost accomplishment of gymnastics, cleared the fence at a leap. The hunter, embarrassed with his rifle and accoutrements, was driven to the slow and humiliating expedient of climbing it. But an outline of the form of the fugitive, fleeting through the shades in the direction of the house, assured him that he had mistaken the species of the game. His heart throbbed from a hundred sensations; and among them an apprehension of the consequences that would have resulted from discharging his rifle, when he had first shined those liquid blue eyes. Seeing that the fleet game made straight in the direction of the house, he said to himself, "I will see the pet deer in its lair;" and he directed his steps to the same place. Half a score of dogs opened their barking upon him, as he approached the house, and advertised the master that a stranger was approaching. Having hushed the dogs, and learned the name of his visitant, he introduced him to his family, as the son of their neighbor, Boone.

Scarce had the first words of introduction been uttered, before the opposite door opened, and a boy apparently of seven, and a girl of sixteen, rushed in, panting for breath and seeming in affright.

"Sister went down to the river, and a *painter* chased her, and she is almost scared to death," exclaimed the boy.

The ruddy, flaxen-haired girl stood full in view of her terrible pursuer, leaning upon his rifle, and surveying her with the most eager admiration. "Rebecca, this is young Boone, son of our neighbor," was their laconic introduction. Both were young, beautiful, and at the period when the affections exercise their most energetic influence. The circumstances of the introduction were favorable to the result, and the young hunter felt that the eyes of the *deer* had *shined* his bosom as fatally as his rifle shot had ever the innocent deer of the thickets. She, too, when she saw the high, open, bold forehead; clear, keen, and yet gentle and affectionate eye --the firm front, and the visible impress of decision and fearlessness of the hunter—when she interpreted a look, which said as distinctly as looks could say it, 'how terrible it would have been to have fired!" can hardly be supposed to have regarded him with indifference. Nor can it be wondered at that she saw in him her *beau ideal* of excellence and beauty. The inhabitants of cities, who live in mansions, and read novels stored with unreal pictures of life and the heart, are apt to imagine that love, with all its golden illusions, is reserved exclusively for them. It is a most egregious mistake. A model of ideal beauty and perfection is woven in almost every youthful heart, of the brightest and most brilliant threads that compose the web of existence. It may not be said that this forest maiden was deeply and foolishly smitten at first sight. All reasonable time and space were granted to the claims of maidenly modesty. As for Boone, he was incurably wounded by her, whose eyes he had *shined*, and as he was remarkable for the backwoods attribute of *never being beaten out of his track*, he ceased not to woo, until he gained the heart of Rebecca Bryan. In a word, he courted her successfully, and they were married.

CHAPTER II.

Boone removes to the head waters of the Yadkin river—He meets with Finley, who had crossed the mountains into Tennessee—They agree to explore the wilderness west of the Alleghanies together.

After his marriage, Boone's first step was to consider where he should find a place, in which he could unite the advantages of fields to cultivate, and range for hunting. True to the impulse of his nature, he plunged deeper into the wilderness, to realize this dream of comfort and happiness. Leaving his wife, he visited the unsettled regions of North Carolina, and selected a spot near the head waters of the Yadkin, for his future home.

The same spirit that afterwards operated to take Mrs. Boone to Kentucky, now led her to leave her friends, and follow her husband to a region where she was an entire stranger. Men change their place of abode from ambition or interest; women from affection. In the course of a few months, Daniel Boone had reared comfortable cabins upon a pleasant eminence at a little distance from the river bank, inclosed a field, and gathered around him the means of abundance and enjoyment. His dwelling, though of rude exterior, offered the weary traveller shelter, a cheerful fire, and a plentiful board, graced with the most cordial welcome. The faces that looked on him were free from the cloud of care. the constraint of ceremony, and the distrust and fear, with which men learn to regard one another in the midst of the rivalry, competition, and scramble of populous cities. The spoils of the chase gave variety to his table, and afforded Boone an excuse for devoting his leisure hours to his favorite pursuit. The country around spread an ample field for its exercise, as it was almost untouched by the axe of the woodsman.

The lapse of a few years—passed in the useful and unpretending occupations of the husbandman—brought no external change to Daniel Boone, deserving of record. His step was now the firm tread of sober manhood; and his purpose the result of matured reflection. This influence of the progress of time, instead of obliterating the original impress of his character, only sunk it deeper. The dwellings of immigrants were springing up in all directions around. Inclosures again began to surround him on every hand, shutting him out from his accustomed haunts in the depths of the forest shade. He saw cultivated fields stretching over large extents of country; and in the distance, villages and towns; and was made sensible of their train of forms, and laws, and restrictions, and buts, and bounds, gradually approaching his habitation. He determined again to leave them far behind. His resolve was made, but he had not decided to what point he would turn. Circumstances soon occurred to terminate his indecision.

As early as 1760, the country west of the Cumberland mountains was considered by the inhabitants of Carolina and Virginia, as involved in something of the same obscurity which lay over the American continent, after its first discovery by Columbus. Those who spread their sails to cross the sea, and find new skies, a new soil, and men in a new world, were not deemed more daring by their brethren at home, than the few hardy adventurers, who struck into the pathless forests stretching along the frontier settlements of the western country, were estimated by their friends and neighbors. Even the most informed and intelligent, where information and intelligence were cultivated, knew so little of the immense extent of country, now designated as the "Mississippi Valley," that a book, published near the year 1800, in Philadelphia or New York, by a writer of talent and standing, speaks of the *many* mouths of the Missouri, as entering the Mississippi *far below the Ohio.*

The simple inmates of cabins, in the remote region bordering on the new country, knew still less about it; as they had not penetrated its wilderness, and were destitute of that general knowledge which prevents the exercise of the exaggerations of vague conjecture. There was, indeed, ample room for the indulgence of speculation upon the features by which the unexplored land was characterized. Its mountains, plains, and streams, animals, and men, were yet to be discovered and named. It might be found the richest land under the sun, exhaustless in fertility, yielding the most valuable productions, and unfailing in its resources. It was possible it would prove a sterile desert. Imagination could not but expatiate in this unbounded field and unexplored wilderness; and there are few persons entirely secure from the influence of imagination. The real danger attending the first exploration of a country filled with wild animals and savages; and the difficulty of carrying a sufficient supply of ammunition to procure food, during a long journey, necessarily made on foot, had prevented any attempt of the kind. The Alleghany mountains had hitherto stood an un surmounted barrier between the Atlantic country and the shores of the beautiful Ohio.

Not far from this period, Dr. Walker, an intelligent and enterprising Virginian, collected a small party, and actually crossed the mountains at the Cumberland Gap, after traversing Powell's valley. One of his leading inducements to this tour, was the hope of making botanical discoveries. The party crossed Cumberland river, and pursued a north-east course over the highlands, which give rise to the sources of the lesser tributaries of the important streams that water the Ohio valley. They reached Big Sandy, after enduring the privations and fatigue incident to such an undertaking. From this point they commenced their return home. On reaching it, they showed no inclination to resume their attempt, although the information thus gained respecting the country, presented it in a very favorable light. These first adventurers wanted the hardihood, unconquerable fortitude, and unwavering purpose, which nothing but death could arrest, that marked the pioneers, who followed in their footsteps. Some time elapsed before a second exploring expedition was set on foot. The relations of what these men had seen on the other side of the mountains had assumed the form of romance, rather than reality. Hunters, alone or in pairs, now ventured to extend their range into the skirts of the wilderness, thus gradually enlarging the sphere of definite conceptions, respecting the country beyond it.

In 1767, a backwoodsman of the name of Finley, of North Carolina, in company with a few kindred spirits resembling him in character, advanced still farther into the interior of the land of promise. It is probable, they chose the season of flowers for their enterprise; as on the return of this little band, a description of the soil they had trodden, and the sights they had seen, went abroad, that charmed all ears, excited all imaginations, and dwelt upon every tongue. Well might they so describe. Their course lay through a portion of Tennessee. There is nothing grand or imposing in scenery—nothing striking or picturesque in cascades and precipitous declivities of mountains covered with woods—nothing romantic and delightful in deep and sheltered valleys, through which wind clear streams, which is not found in this first region they traversed. The mountains here stretch along in continuous ridges—and there shoot up into elevated peaks. On the summits of some, spread plateaus, which afford the most commanding prospects, and offer all advantages for cultivation, overhung by the purest atmosphere. No words can picture the secluded beauty of some of the vales bordering the creeks and small streams, which dash transparent as air over rocks, moss-covered and time-worn—walled in by the precipitous sides of mountains. down which pour numberless waterfalls.

The soil is rich beyond any tracts of the same character in the west. Beautiful white, gray, and red marbles are found here; and sometimes fine specimens of rock-crystals. Salt springs abound. It has lead mines; and iron ore is no where more abundant. Its salt-petre caves are most astonishing curiosities. One of them has been traced ten miles. Another, on a high point of Cumberland mountain, has a perpendicular descent, the bottom of which has never been sounded. They abound in prodigious vaulted apartments and singular chambers, the roofs springing up into noble arches, or running along for miles in regular oblong excavations. The gloomy grandeur, produced by the faint illumination of torches in these immense subterranean retreats, may be imagined, but not described. Springs rise, and considerable streams flow through them, on smooth limestone beds.

This is the very home of subterranean wonders, showing the noblest caves in the world. In comparison with them, the celebrated one at Antiparos is but a slight excavation. Spurs of the mountains, called the "Enchanted Mountains," show traces impressed in the solid limestone, of the footsteps of men, horses, and other animals, as distinctly as though they had been made upon clay mortar. In places the tracks are such as would be made by feet, that had slidden upon soft clay in descending declivities.

Prodigious remains of animals are found near the

salines. Whole trees are discovered completely petrified; and to crown the list of wonders, in turning up the soil, graves are opened, which contain the skeletons of figures, who must have been of mature age. Paintings of the sun, moon, animals, and serpents, on high and apparently inaccessible cliffs, out of question the work of former ages, in colors as fresh as if recently laid on, and in some instances, just and ingenious in delineation, are a subject of untiring speculation. Even the streams in this region of wonders have scooped out for themselves immensely deep channels hemmed in by perpendicular walls of limestone, sometimes springing up to a height of three or four hundred feet. As the traveller looks down upon the dark waters rolling so far beneath him, seeming to flow in a subterranean world, he cannot but feel impressions of the grandeur of nature stealing over him.

It is not to be supposed, that persons, whose sole object in entering the country was to explore it, would fail to note these surprising traces of past races, the beautiful diversity of the aspect of the country, or these wonders of nature exhibited on every hand. Being neither incurious nor incompetent observers, their delineations were graphic and vivid.

> "Their teachers had been woods and rills,
> The silence, that is in the starry sky;
> The sleep, that is among the lonely hills."

They advanced into Kentucky so far, as to fill their imaginations with the fresh and luxuriant beauty of its lawns. its rich cane-brakes and flowering forests To them it was a terrestrial paradise; for it was full of game. Deer, elk, bears, buffaloes, panthers, wolves, wild-cats, and foxes, abounded in the thick tangles of the green cane; and in the open woods, pheasants, partridges, and turkeys, were as plenty as domestic fowls in the old settlements.

Such were the materials, from which these hunters, on their return formed descriptions that fixed in the remembrance, and operated upon the fancy of all who heard. A year after Finley's return, his love of wandering led him into the vicinity of Daniel Boone. They met, and the hearts of these kindred spirits at once warmed towards each other. Finley related his adventures, and painted the delights of *Kain-tuck-kee*—for such was its Indian name. Boone had but few hair-breath escapes to recount, in comparison with his new companion. But it can readily be imagined, that a burning sensation rose in his breast, like that of the celebrated painter Correggio, when low-born, untaught, poor and destitute of every advantage, save that of splendid native endowment, he stood before the work of the immortal Raphael, and said, "I too am a painter!" Boone's purpose was fixed. In a region, such as Finley described, far in advance of the wearying monotony of a life of inglorious toil, he would have space to roam unwitnessed, undisturbed by those of his own race, whose only thought was to cut down trees, at least for a period of some years. We wish not to be understood to laud these views, as wise or just. In the order of things, however, it was necessary, that men like Finley and Boone, and their companions, should precede in the wilderness, to prepare the way for the multitudes who would soon follow. It is probable, that no motives but those ascribed to them, would have induced these adventurers to face the hardships and extremes of suffering from exposure and hunger, and the peril of life, which they literally carried in their hand.

No feeling, but a devotion to their favorite pursuits and modes of life, stronger than the fear of abandonment, in the interminable and pathless woods, to all forms of misery and death, could ever have enabled them to persist in braving the danger and distress that stared them in the face at every advancing step.

Finley was invited by Boone permanently to share the comfort of his fire-side,—for it was now winter. It needs no exercise of fancy to conjecture their subjects of conversation during the long evening. The bitter wintry wind burst upon their dwelling only to enhance the cheerfulness of the blazing fire in the huge chimneys, by the contrast of the inclemency of nature without.

It does not seem natural, at first thought, that a season, in which nature shows herself stern and unrelenting, should be chosen, as that in which plans are originated and matured for settling the destiny of life. But it was during this winter, that Boone and Finley arranged all the preliminaries of their expedition, and agreed to meet on the first of May in the coming spring; and with some others, whom they hoped to induce to join them for greater strength and safety, to set forth together on an expedition into Kentucky.

Boone's array of arguments, to influence those whom he wished to share this daring enterprise with him, was tinctured with the coloring of rude poetry. "They would ascend," he said, "the unnamed mountains, whose green heads rose not far from their former hunting-grounds, since fences and inclosures had begun to surround them on all sides, shutting up the hunter from his free range and support. The deer had fled from the sound of the axe, which levelled the noble trees under whose shade they could repose from the fatigues of pursuit. The springs and streams among the hills were bared to the fierce sun, and would soon dry up and disappear. Soon 'the horn would no more wake them up in the morn.' The sons of their love and pride, instead of being trained hunters, with a free, bold step, frank kindness, true honor, and a courage that knew not fear, would become men to whom the pleasures and dangers of their fathers would seem an idle tale." The prospect spreading on the other side of the mountains, he pictured as filled with all the images of abundance and freedom that could enter the thoughts of the hunter. The paintings were drawn from nature, and the words few and simple, that spoke to the hearts of these sons of the forest. "The broad woods," he pursued, "would stretch beneath their eyes, when the mountain summits were gained, one extended tuft of blossoms. The cane was a tangle of luxuriance, affording the richest pastures. The only paths through it were those made by buffaloes and bears. In the sheltered glades, turkeys and large wild birds were so abundant, that a hunter could supply himself in an hour for the wants of a week. They would not be found like the lean and tough birds in the old settlements, that lingered around the clearings and stumps of the trees, in the topmost of whose branches the fear of man compelled them to rest, but young and full fed. The trees in this new land were of no stinted or gnarled growth, but shot up tall, straight, and taper. The yellow poplar here threw up into the air a column of an hundred feet shaft in a contest with the sycamore for the pre-eminence of the woods. Their wives and children would remain safe in their present homes, until the first dangers and fatigues of the new settlement had been met and overcome. When their homes were selected, and their cabins built, they would return and bring them out to their new abodes. The outward journey could be regulated by the uncontrolled pleasure of their more frail travellers. What guardians could be more true than their husbands with their good rifles and the skill and determination to use them? They would depend, not upon circumstances, but upon themselves. The babes would exult in the arms of their mothers from the inspiring influence of the fresh air; and at night a cradle from the hollow tree would rock them to a healthful repose. The older children, training to the pursuits and pleasures of a life in the woods, and acquiring vigor of body and mind with every day, in their season of prime, would feel no shame that they had hearts softened by the warm current of true feeling. When their own silver hairs lay thin upon the brow, and their eye was dim, and sounds came confused on their ear, and their step faltered, and their form bent, they would find consideration, and care, and tenderness from children, whose breasts were not steeled by ambition, nor hardened by avarice; in whom the beautiful influences of the indulgence of none but natural desires and pure affections would not be deadened by the selfishness, vanity, and fear of ridicule, that are the harvest of what is called *civilized and cultivated* life." Such at least, in after life, were the contrasts that Boone used to present between social life and that of the woodsman.

CHAPTER III.

Boone, with Finley and others, start on their exploring expedition — Boone kills a panther in the night—Their progress over the mountains—They descend into the great valley—Description of the new country—Herds of buffaloes—Their wanderings in the wilderness.

THE first of May, 1769, Finley and Boone, with four others, whose names were Stewart, Holden, Mooney, and Cool, and who had pledged themselves to the undertaking, were assembled at the house of Boone, in readiness to commence their journey. It may be imagined that all the neighbors gathered to witness their departure. A rifle, ammunition, and a light knapsack were all the baggage with which they dared encumber themselves. Provisions for a few days were bestowed along with the clothing deemed absolutely necessary for comfort upon the long route. No shame could attach to the manhood and courage of Daniel Boone from the fact that tears were said to have rushed to his eyes, as he kissed his wife and children before he turned from his door for the last time for months, and perhaps forever. The nature of the pioneer was as gentle and affectionate as it was firm and persevering. He had power, however, to send back the unbidden gush to its source, and forcibly to withdraw his mind from enervating thoughts.

Beside, the natural elasticity of his temperament and the buoyancy of his character came to his aid. The anticipation of new and strange incidents operated to produce in the minds of the travellers, from the commencement of the enterprise, a kind of wild pleasure.

With alert and vigorous steps they pursued a north-west course, and were soon beyond the reach of the most distant view of their homes. This day and night, and the succeeding one, the scenes in view were familiar; but in the course of the four or five that followed, all vestiges of civilized habitancy had disappeared. The route lay through a solitary and trackless wilderness. Before them rose a line of mountains, shooting up against the blue of the horizon, in peaks and elevations of all forms. The slender store of food with which they had set out, was soon exhausted. To obtain a fresh supply was the first and most pressing want. Accordingly, a convenient place was selected, and a camp constructed of logs and branches of trees, to keep out the dew and rain. The whole party joined in this preliminary arrangement. When it was so far completed, as to enable a part to finish it before night-fall, part of the company took their rifles and went in different directions in pursuit of game. They returned in time for supper, with a couple of deer and some wild turkeys. Those, whose business it was to finish the camp, had made a generous fire and acquired keen appetites for the coming feast. The deer were rapidly dressed, so far at least as to furnish a supper of venison. It had not been long finished, and the arrangements for the night made, before the clouds, which had been gathering blackness for some hours, rolled up in immense folds from the point, whence was heard the sudden burst of a furious wind. The lightning darted from all quarters of the heavens. At one moment every object stood forth in a glare of dazzling light. The next the darkness might almost be felt. The rain fell in torrents, in one apparently unbroken sheet from the sky to the earth. The peals of thunder rolled almost unheard amid this deafening rush of waters. The camp of the travellers, erected with reference to the probability of such an occurrence, was placed under the shelter of a huge tree, whose branches ran out laterally, and were of a thickness of foliage to be almost impervious to the rain. To this happy precaution of the woodsmen, they owed their escape from the drenching of the shower. They were not, perhaps, aware of the greater danger from lightning, to which their position had exposed them.

As was the universal custom in cases like theirs, a watch was kept by two, while the others slept. The watches were relieved several times during the night. About midnight, Boone and Holden being upon the watch, the deep stillness abroad was broken by a shrill scream, resembling the shriek of a frightened woman or child more nearly than any other sound. The two companions had been sitting in a contemplative mood, listening to the deep breathing of the sleepers, when this cry came upon their ears. Both sprang erect. "What is that?" exclaimed Holden, who was not an experienced backwoodsman, in comparison with the others. "Hush!" answered Boone; "do not wake the rest.

It is nothing but the cry of a panther. Take your gun and come with me."

They stole gently from the camp and listened in breathless silence for a repetition of the cry. It was soon repeated, indicating the place where the animal was. Groping cautiously through the bushes in its direction, frequently stopping to look around, and holding their rifles ready for an instantaneous shot, they drew near the formidable animal. At length they discovered at a little distance before them, two balls that glared with an intense brightness, like that of living coals of fire. Boone, taking deliberate aim, in the best manner that the darkness would permit, discharged his rifle. The yell of pain from the animal, as it was heard leaping among the undergrowth in an opposite direction, satisfied Boone that his shot had taken sufficient effect to prevent a second disturbance from it, at least for that night, and he returned to the camp with his companion. The sleepers, aroused by the report of the gun, were awaiting him. The account of the adventure afforded speculation, touching the point, whether the animal had been killed or would return again. Early the next morning, some were dispatched to bring in more game, while others prepared and dried what had already been obtained. The whole day was spent in this way, and the night following passed without any disturbance.

With the first light of the sun on the succeeding morning, they threw their knapsacks over their shoulders, and leaving their temporary shelter to benefit any who might come after them, resumed their route. They had not proceeded far before an animal stretched on the ground attracted attention. It was a dead panther. By comparing the size of the ball, which had killed it, with those used by Boone, the party were satisfied that this was the same animal he had shot the night after the storm.

During the day they began the ascent of the ridge of the Alleghany, that had for some days bounded their view. The mountainous character of the country, for some miles, before the highest elevations rose to sight, rendered the travelling laborious and slow. Several days were spent in this toilsome progress. Steep summits, impossible to ascend, impeded their advance, compelling them to turn aside, and attain the point above by a circuitous route. Again they were obliged to delay their journey for a day, in order to obtain a fresh supply of provisions. This was readily procured, as all the varieties of game abounded on every side.

The last crags and cliffs of the middle ridges having been scrambled over, on the following morning they stood on the summit of Cumberland mountain, the farthest western spur of this line of heights. From this point the descent into the great western valley began. What a scene opened before them! A feeling of the sublime is inspired in every bosom susceptible of it, by a view from any point of these vast ranges, of the boundless forest valleys of the Ohio. It is a view more grand, more heart-stirring than that of the ocean. Illimitable extents of wood, and winding river courses spread before them like a large map. "Glorious country!" they exclaimed. Little did Boone dream that in fifty years, immense portions of it would pass from the domain of the hunter—that it would contain four millions of freemen, and its waters be navigated by nearly two hundred steam boats, sweeping down these streams that now rolled through the unbroken forests before them. To them it stood forth an unexplored paradise of the hunter's imagination.

After a long pause, in thoughts too deep for words. they began the descent, which was made in a much shorter time than had been required for the opposite ascent; and the explorers soon found themselves on the slopes of the subsiding hills. Here the hunter was in his element. To all the party but Finley, the buffaloes incidentally seen in small numbers in the valleys, were a novel and interesting sight. It had as yet been impossible to obtain a shot at them, from their distance or position. It may be imagined with what eagerness Boone sought an opportunity to make his first essay in this exciting and noble species of hunting.

The first considerable drove came in sight on the afternoon of the day on which the travellers reached the foot of the mountains. The day had been one of the most beautiful of spring. The earth was covered with grass of the freshest green. The rich foliage of the trees, in its varied shading, furnished its portion of the loveliness of the surrounding landscape. The light of the declining sun lay full on the scene of boundless solitude. The party had descended into a deep glen, which wound through the opening between the highlands, still extending a little in advance of them. They pursued its course until it terminated in a beautiful little plain. Upon advancing into this, they found themselves in an area of considerable extent, almost circular in form, bounded on one half its circumference by the line of hills, from among which they had just emerged. The other sections of the circle were marked by the fringe of wood that bordered a stream winding from the hills, at a considerable distance above. The buffaloes advanced from the skirt of wood, and the plain was soon filled by the moving mass of these huge animals.

The exploring adventurers perceived themselves in danger of what has more than once happened in similar situations. The prospect seemed to be that they would be trampled under the feet of the reckless and sweeping body, in their onward course.

"They will not turn out for us," said Finley; "and if we do not conduct exactly right, we shall be crushed to death."

The inexperienced adventurers bade him direct them in the emergency. Just as the front of the phalanx was within short rifle distance, he discharged his rifle and brought down one of the bulls, that seemed to be a file leader, by a ball between the horns. The unwieldy animal fell. The mass raised a deafening sort of bellow, and became arrested, as if transfixed to the spot. A momentary confusion of the mass behind ensued. But, borne along by the pressure of the multitudes still in the rear, there was a gradual parting of the herd direct from the front, where the fallen buffalo lay. The disruption once made, the chasm broadened, until when the wings passed the travellers, they were thirty yards from the divisions on either hand. To prevent the masses yet behind from closing their lines, Finley took the rifle of one of his companions, and levelled another. This changed the pace of the animals to a rout. The last masses soon thundered by, and left them gazing in astonishment, not unmixed with joy, in realizing their escape. "Job of Uz," exclaimed Boone, "had not larger droves of cattle than we. In fact, we seem to have had in this instance an abundance to a fault."

As this was an era in their adventures, and an omen of the abundance of the vast regions of forests which they had descried from the summits of the mountains, they halted, made a camp, and skinned the animals, preserving the skins, fat, tongues, and choice pieces. No epicures ever feasted higher than these athletic and hungry hunters, as they sat around their evening fire, and commented upon the ease with which their wants would be supplied in a country thus abounding with such animals.

After feasting again in the morning on the spoils of the preceding day, and packing such parts of the animals as their probable necessities suggested, they commenced their march; and in no great distance reached Red river, a branch of the Cumberland. They followed the meanders of this river for some miles, until they reached, on the 7th day of June,

Finley's former station, where his preceding explorations of the western country had terminated.

Their journey to this point had lasted more than a month; and though the circumstances in which they had made it, had been generally auspicious, so long a route through unknown forests, and over precipitous mountains, hitherto untrodden by white men, could not but have been fatiguing in the extreme. None but such spirits could have sustained their hardships without a purpose to turn back, and leave their exploration unaccomplished.

They resolved in this place to encamp, and remain for a time sufficient to recruit themselves for other expeditions and discoveries. The weather had been for some time past, and still remained, rainy and unpleasant; and it became necessary that their station should be of such a construction, as to secure them a dry sleeping place from the rain. The game was so abundant, that they found it a pleasure, rather than a difficulty, to supply themselves with food. The buffaloes were seen like herds of cattle, dispersed among the cane-brakes, or feeding on the grass, or ruminating in the shade. Their skins were of great utility, in furnishing them with moccasins, and many necessary articles indispensable to their comfortable subsistence at their station.

What struck them with unfailing pleasure was, to observe the soil, in general, of a fertility without example on the other side of the mountains. From an eminence in the vicinity of their station, they could see, as far as vision could extend, the beautiful country of Kentucky. They remarked with astonishment the tall, straight trees, shading the exuberant soil, wholly clear from any other underbrush than the rich cane-brakes, the image of verdure and luxuriance, or tall grass and clover. Down the gentle slopes murmured clear limestone brooks. Finley who had some touch of scripture knowledge, exclaimed in view of this wilderness-paradise, so abundant in game and wild fowls, "This wilderness blossoms as the rose; and these desolate places are as the garden of God."

"Ay," responded Boone; "and who would remain on the sterile pine hills of North Carolina, to hear the screaming of the jay, and now and then bring down a deer too lean to be eaten? This is the land of hunters, where man and beast will grow to their full size."

They ranged through various forests, and crossed the numerous streams of the vicinity. By following the paths of the buffaloes, bears, deer, and other animals, they discovered the Salines or *Licks*, where salt is made at the present day. The paths, in approaching the salines, were trodden as hard and smooth, as in the vicinity of the farm-yards of the old settlements. Boone, from the principle which places the best pilot at the helm in a storm, was not slow to learn from innumerable circumstances which would have passed unnoticed by a less sagacious woodsman, that, although the country was not actually inhabited by Indians, it was not the less a scene of strife and combat for the possession of such rich hunting grounds by a great number of tribes. He discovered that it was a common park to these fierce tribes; and none the less likely to expose them to the dangers of Indian warfare, because it was not claimed or inhabited by any particular tribe. On the contrary, instead of having to encounter a single tribe in possession, he foresaw that the jealousy of all the tribes would be united against the new intruders.

These fearless spirits, who were instinctively imbued with an abhorrence of the Indians, heeded little, however, whether they had to make war on them, or the wild beasts. They felt in its fullest force that indomitable elasticity of character, which causes the possessor, every where, and in all forms of imagined peril, to feel sufficient to themselves. Hence the lonely adventurers continued fearlessly to explore the beautiful positions for settlements, to cross and name the rivers, and to hunt.

By a happy fatality, through all the summer they met with no Indians, and experienced no impediment in the way of the most successful hunting. During the season, they had collected large quantities of peltries, and meeting with nothing to excite apprehension or alarm, they became constantly more delighted with the country.

So passed their time, until the 22d of December. After this period adventures of the most disastrous character began to crowd upon them. We forthwith commence the narrative of incidents which constitute the general color of Boone's future life.

CHAPTER IV

The exploring party divide into different routes—Boone and Stewart taken prisoners by the Indians, and their escape—Boone meets with his elder brother and another white man in the woods—Stewart killed by the Indians, and the companion of the elder Boone destroyed by wolves—The elder brother returns to North Carolina, leaving Boone alone in the wilderness.

In order to extend the means of gaining more exact information with regard to this beautiful country, the party divided, and took different directions. Boone and Stewart formed one division, and the remaining three the other. The two former had as yet seen few thick forests. The country was much of it of that description, now known by the name of "Barrens," or open woods, which had the appearance of having been planted out with trees at wide and regular distances from each other, like those of an orchard, allowing the most luxuriant growth of cane, grass, or clover beneath them. They now passed a wide and deep forest, in which the trees were large and thick. Among them were many of the laurel tribe, in full verdure in mid winter. Others were thick hung with persimmons, candied by the frost, nutritive, and as luscious as figs. Others again were covered with winter grapes. Every thing tended to inspire them with exalted notions of the natural resources of the country, and to give birth to those extravagant romances, which afterwards became prevalent, as descriptions of Kentucky. Such were Finley's accounts of it—views which went abroad, and created even in Europe an impression of a kind of new El Dorado, or rather rural paradise. Other and very different scenes, in no great length of time, disenchanted the new paradise, and presented it in the sober traits of truth.

They were never out of sight of buffaloes, deer, and turkeys. At night-fall they came in view of Kentucky river, and admired in unsated astonishment, the precipices three hundred feet high, at the foot of which, as in a channel cut out of the solid limestone, rolled the dark waters of the beautiful stream. A lofty eminence was before them. Thinking it would afford them a far view of the meanderings of the river, they ascended it. This expectation was realized. A large extent of country stretched beneath them. Having surveyed it, they proposed to commence their return to rejoin their companions. As they were leisurely descending the hill, little dreaming of danger, the Indian yell burst upon their ears. A numerous party of Indians sprang from the cane-brake, surrounded, vanquished, and bound them, before they had time to have recourse to their arms. The Indians proceeded to plunder them of their rifles, and every thing in their possession but the most indispensable articles of dress. They then led them off to their camp, where they confined them in such a manner as effectually to prevent their escape.

Not knowing a word of the speech of their captors, who knew as little of theirs, they were wholly ignorant of what fate awaited them. The Indians next day marched them off rapidly towards the north, compelling them to travel at a rate which was excessively annoying to captives in their predicament—manacled, in momentary apprehension of death, and plunging deeper into the wilderness in advancing towards the permanent abode of their savage masters. It was well for them that they were more athletic than the savages, equally capable of endurance, and alike incapable of betraying groans, fear, or even marks of regret in their countenance. They knew enough of savage modes to beware that the least indications of weariness, and inability to proceed, would have brought the tomahawk and scalping-knife upon their skulls—weapons with which they were thus early supplied from Detroit. They therefore pushed resolutely on, with cheerful countenances, watching the while with intense earnestness, to catch from the signs and gestures of the Indians, what was their purpose in regard to their fate. By the second day, they comprehended the words of most frequent recurrence in the discussion, that took place respecting them. Part, they perceived, were for putting them to death to prevent their escape. The other portion advocated their being adopted into the tribe, and domesticated. To give efficacy to the counsels of these last, the captives not only concealed every trace of chagrin, but dissembled cheerfulness, and affected to like their new mode of life; and seemed as happy, and as much amused, as the Indians themselves

Fortunately, their previous modes of life, and in fact their actual aptitudes and propensities wonderfully qualified them, along with their reckless courage and elasticity of character, to enact this difficult part with a success, which completely deceived the Indians, and gave the entire ascendency to the advice of those who proposed to spare, and adopt them into their tribe. Lulled by this semblance, the captors were less and less strict in their guard. On the seventh night of their captivity, the savages, having made a great fire, and fed plentifully, all fell into a sound sleep, leaving their prisoners, who affected to be as deeply asleep as themselves, wholly unguarded.

It need hardly be said, that the appearance of content they had worn, was mere outward show; and that they slept not. Boone slowly and cautiously raised himself to a sitting posture, and thus remained a few moments to mark, if his change of position had been observed. One of the sleepers turned in his sleep. Boone instantly dropped back to his recumbent posture and semblance of sleep. So he remained fifteen minutes, when he once more raised himself, and continued sitting for some time, without noting a movement among the slumberers around him. He then ventured to communicate his purpose to his companion.

The greatest caution was necessary to prevent disturbing the savages, as the slightest noise would awake them, and probably bring instant death upon the captives. Stewart succeeded in placing himself upon his feet without any noise. The compan ions were not far apart, but did not dare to whisper to each other the thought that occurred alike to both—that, should they escape without rifles and ammunition, they must certainly die of hunger. The place where their rifles stood had been carefully noted by them, and by groping their way with the utmost care, they finally reached them. Fortunately, the equipments, containing the usual supply of powder and ball, were near the rifles. The feelings with which Boone and Stewart stole forth from the circle of their captors may be imagined. They made their way into the woods through the darkness, keeping close together for some time, before they exchanged words.

It was not far from morning when they began their attempt at escape; but they had made considerable progress from the Indian encampment before the dawn. They took their course with the first light, and pursued it the whole day, reaching their camp without meeting with any accident. As the sun was declining, forms were seen approaching the camp in the distance. The uncertain light in which they were first visible, rendered it impossible for Boone and Stewart to determine whether they were whites or Indians; but they grasped their rifles, and stood ready for defence. The forms continued to approach cautiously and slowly, until they were within speaking distance. Boone then hailed them with the challenge, "Who comes there?" The delight may be imagined with which Boone and Stewart heard the reply of "White men and friends!" "Come on then," said Boone. The next moment he found himself in the arms of his brother, who, accompanied by a single companion, had left North Carolina, and made his way all the distance from the Yadkin to the Cumberland They had been wandering many days in the woods. in pursuit of Boone and his party, and had thus providentially fallen upon them.

Notwithstanding the damp which it must cast on the spirits of these new adventurers to hear of the recent captivity of Boone and Stewart, and the uncertain fate of the rest of the company, this joyous meeting of brothers and friends in the wilderness, and this intelligence from home, filled the parties with a joy too sincere and unalloyed to be repressed by apprehensions for the future.

The four associates commenced the usual occupation of hunting, but were soon alarmed by signs of the vicinity of Indians, and clear proofs that they were prowling near them in the woods. These circumstances strongly admonished them not to venture singly to any great distance from each other. In the eagerness of pursuing a wounded buffalo, Boone and Stewart, however, allowed themselves to be separated from their companions. Aware of their imprudence, and halting to return, a party of savages rushed from the cane-brake, and discharged a shower of arrows upon them, one of which laid Stewart dead on the spot. The first purpose of Boone was to fire upon them, and sell his life as dearly as possible. But rashness is not bravery; and seeing the numbers of the foe, the hopelessness of resistance, and the uselessness of bartering his own life for the revenge of inflicting a single death—reflecting, moreover, on the retaliation it would probably bring down on the remainder of his companions, he retreated, and escaped, amidst a flight of arrows, in safety to the camp.

One would have supposed that this party would have needed no more monition to keep them together, and always on their guard. But, forgetful of the fate of Stewart, the partner of the elder Boone, who had recently arrived, allowed himself to be beguiled away from the two Boones, as they were hunting together. The object of his curiosity was of little importance. In pursuit of it, he wandered into a swamp, and was lost. The two brothers sought him, long and painfully, to no purpose. Discouraged, and perhaps exasperated in view of his careless imprudence, they finally concluded he had chosen that method of deserting them, and had set out on his return to North Carolina. Under such impressions, they relinquished the search, and returned to camp. They had reason afterwards to repent their harsh estimate of his intentions. Fragments of his clothes, and traces of blood were found on the opposite side of the swamp. A numerous pack of wolves had been heard to howl in that direction the evening on which he had been lost. Circumstances placed it beyond a doubt, that, while wandering about in search of his companions, these terrible animals had come upon him and torn him in pieces. He was never heard of afterwards.

The brothers were thus left alone in this wide wilderness, the only white men west of the mountains; as they concluded the remainder of the original party had returned to North Carolina. But they were neither desponding nor indolent. They held pleasant communion together—hunted by day, cooked their game, sat by their bright fires, and sung the airs of their country by night, as though in the midst of the gayest society. They devoted, beside, much of their time and labor to preparing a comfortable cabin to shelter them during the approaching winter.

They were in want of many things. Clothing and moccasins they might supply. With bread, sugar, and salt, though articles of the first necessity, they could dispense. But ammunition, an article absolutely indispensable, was failing them. They concluded, too, that horses would be of essential service to them. They finally came to the resolution that the elder Boone should return to North Carolina, and come out to the new country with ammunition, horses, and supplies.

The character of Daniel Boone, in consenting to be left alone in that wilderness, surrounded by perils from the Indians and wild beasts, of which he had so recently and terribly been made aware, appears in its true light. We have heard of a Robinson Crusoe made so by the necessity of shipwreck; but all history can scarcely parallel another such an instance of a man voluntarily consenting to be left alone among savages and wild beasts, seven hundred miles from the nearest white inhabitant. The separation came. The elder brother disappeared in the forest, and Daniel Boone was left in the cabin, so recently cheered by the presence of his brother, entirely alone. Their only dog followed the departing brother, and Boone had nothing but his unconquerable spirit to sustain him during the long and lonely days and nights, visited by the remembrance of his distant wife and children.

To prevent the recurrence of dark and lonely thoughts, he set out, soon after his brother left him, on a distant excursion to the north-west. The country grew still more charming under his eye at every step of his advance. He wandered through the delightful country of the Barrens, and gained the heights of one of the ridges of Salt river, whence he could look back on the Alleghany ridges, lifting their blue heads in the direction of the country of his wife and children. Before him rolled the majestic Ohio, down its dark forests, and seen by him for the first time. It may be imagined what thoughts came over his mind, as the lonely hunter stood on the shore of this mighty stream, straining his thoughts towards its sources, and the unknown country where it discharged itself into some other river, or the sea. During this journey he explored the country on the south shore of the Ohio, between the Cumberland and the present site of Louisville, experiencing in these lonely explorations a strange pleasure, which, probably, none but those of his temperament can adequately imagine.

Returning to his cabin, as a kind of head quarters, he found it undisturbed by the Indians. Caution suggested to him the expedient of often changing his position, and not continuing permanently to sleep in the cabin. Sometimes he slept in the cane-brake, sometimes under the covert of a limestone cliff, often made aware on his return to the cabin that the Indians had discovered it, and visited it during his absence. Surrounded with danger and death, though insensible to fear, he neglected none of those prudent precautions of which men of his temperament are much more able to avail themselves, than those always forecasting the fashion of uncertain evils. He was, however, never for an hour in want of the most ample supply of food. Herds of deer and buffaloes were seldom out of his sight for a day together. His nights were often disturbed by the howling of wolves, which abounded as much as the other forest animals. His table thus abundantly spread in the wilderness, and every excursion affording new views of the beautiful solitudes, he used to affirm afterwards that this period was among the happiest in his life; that during it, care and melancholy, and a painful sense of loneliness, were alike unknown to him.

We must not, however, suppose that the lonely hunter was capable only of feeling the stern and sullen pleasures of the savage. On the contrary, he was a man of the kindliest nature, and of the tenderest affections. We have read of verses, in solid columns, said to have been made by him. We would be sorry to believe him the author of these verses, for they would redound little to his honor as a poet. But, though we believe he did not attempt to make bad verses, the woodsman was essentially a poet. He loved nature in all her aspects of beauty and grandeur with the intensest admiration. He never wearied of admiring the charming natural landscapes spread before him; and, to his latest days, his spirit in old age seemed to revive in the season of spring, and when he visited the fires of the sugar camps, blazing in the open maple groves.

CHAPTER V.

Boone is pursued by the Indians, and eludes their pursuit—He encounters and kills a bear—The return of his brother with ammunition—They explore the country—Boone kills a panther on the back of a buffalo—They return to North Carolina.

Boone's brother had departed on the first of May. During the period of his absence, which lasted until the twenty-second of July, he considered himself the only white person west of the mountains. It is true, some time in this year, (1770,) probably in the latter part of it, an exploring party led by General James Knox, crossed the Alleghany mountains. But this exploring expedition confined its discoveries principally to the country south and west of the river Kentucky. This exploration was desultory, and without much result. Boone never met with them, or knew that they were in the country. Consequently, in regard to his own estimation, he was as completely alone in this unexplored world, as though they had not been there.

He never allowed himself to neglect his caution in respect to the numerous savages spread over the country. He knew that he was exposed every moment to the danger of falling into their hands. The fate of Stewart had served as a warning to him. It is wonderful that he should have been able to traverse such an extent of country as he did, and live in it so many months, and yet evade them. It required no little ingenuity and self-possession to take such measures as insured this good fortune.

About mid-day, near the close of the month of June, he paused in one of his excursions for a short time under the shade of a tree. As he looked cautiously around him, he perceived four Indians advancing openly towards him, but at a considerable distance, and apparently without having yet seen him. He did not delay to recommence his course through the woods, hoping by short turns, and concealing himself among the hills, to prevent an encounter with them, as the chance of four to one was too great an odds against him. He advanced in this way one or two miles; but as he cast a glance behind, he saw, with pain, that they sedulously followed in his trail at nearly their first distance, showing the same perseverance and sagacity of pursuit with which a hound follows a deer. When he first perceived them, he was in such a position that he could see them, and yet remain himself unseen. He was convinced that they had not discovered his person, although so closely pursued by them. But how to throw them off his trail, he was at a loss to conjecture. He adopted a number of expedients in succession, but saw the Indians still on the track behind. Suddenly a method occurred to his imagination, which finally proved successful. Large grape vines swung from the trees in all directions around him.

Hastening onward at a more rapid pace, until he passed a hill that would serve to conceal him for a few moments, he seized a vine sufficiently strong to support his weight; and disengaging it from the roots, climbed it a few feet, by bracing against the tree to which it was attached. When he had attained the necessary height, he gave himself so strong an impulse from the tree, that he reached the ground some yards from the spot where he left it. By this expedient he broke his trail.

Resuming his route in a course at right angles from that he had previously followed, as fast as possible, he finally succeeded in entirely distancing his pursuers, and leaving them at fault in pursuing his trail.

Boone soon after this met with a second adventure in which he actually encountered a foe scarcely less formidable than the savage. Rendered doubly watchful by his late escape, none of the forest sounds escaped his notice. Hearing the approach of what he judged to be a large animal by the noise of its movement through the cane, he held his rifle ready for instant use, and drew from its sheath a long and sharp knife, which he always wore in his belt. He determined to try the efficacy of his rifle first. As the animal came in sight it proved to be a she bear. They are exceedingly ferocious at all times, and their attack is dangerous and often fatal; but particularly so, when they are surrounded by their cubs, as was the case in this instance.

As soon as the animal perceived him it gave indications of an intention to make battle. Boone levelled his rifle, and remained quiet, until the bear was sufficiently near to enable him to shoot with effect. In general his aim was sure; but this time the ball did not reach the point at which he had aimed; and

the wound it inflicted only served to render the animal mad with rage and pain. It was impossible for him to reload and discharge his gun a second time before it would reach him; and yet he did not relish the idea of grappling with it in close fight. His knife was the resource to which he instantly turned. He held it in his right hand in such a position that the bear could not reach his person without receiving its point. His rifle, held in his left hand, served as a kind of shield. Thus prepared, he awaited the onset of the formidable animal. When within a foot of him, it reared itself erect to grasp him with its huge paws. In this position it pressed upon the knife until the whole blade was buried in its body. Boone had pointed it directly to the heart of the animal. It fell harmless to the ground.

The time fixed for the return of his brother was drawing near. Extreme solicitude respecting him now disturbed the hitherto even tenor of his life. He remained most of his time in his cabin, hunting no more than was necessary for subsistence, and then in the direction in which his brother would be likely to approach. It was not doubt of his brother's compliance with his promise of return, that disturbed the woodsman—such a feeling never even entered his mind. He was confident he would prove faithful to the trust reposed in him; but the difficulties and dangers of the way were so great for a solitary individual upon the route before him, that Boone feared he might fall a victim to them, notwithstanding the utmost exertion of self-possession and fortitude.

Day after day passed, after the extreme limit of the period fixed by the elder Boone for his return, and still he came not. It may be imagined that Boone had need of all the firmness and philosophy of character, with which he was so largely endowed by nature, to sustain him under the pressure of anxiety for the safety of his brother, and to hear through him from his family. He suffered, too, from the conviction that he must soon starve in the wilderness himself, as his ammunition was almost gone. He could not hope to see his family again, unless his brother or some other person furnished him the means of obtaining food on his way to rejoin them. His rifle—his dependence for subsistence and defence—would soon become entirely useless. What to others would have been real dangers and trials—a solitary life in the wilderness, exposure to the attacks of the savages and wild beasts—were regarded by him as nothing; but here he saw himself driven to the last extremity, and without resource. These meditations, although they made him thoughtful, did not dispirit him. His spirit was unconquerable. He was sitting one evening, near sunset, at the door of his cabin, indulging in reflections naturally arising from his position. His attention was withdrawn by a sound as of something approaching through the forest. Looking up, he saw nothing, but he arose, and stood prepared for defence. He could now distinguish the sound as of horses advancing directly towards the cabin. A moment afterwards he saw, through the trees, his brother mounted on one horse, and leading another heavily laden.

It would be useless to attempt to describe his sensations at this sight. Every one will feel instantly, how it must have operated upon all the sources of joy. More unmixed happiness is seldom enjoyed on the earth, than that, in which the brothers spent this evening. His brother brought him good news of the health and welfare of his family, and of the affectionate remembrance in which he was held by them; and an abundant supply of ammunition, beside many other articles, that in his situation, might be deemed luxuries. The brothers talked over their supper, and until late at night, for they had much to relate to each other, and both had been debarred the pleasure of conversation so long that it now seemed as though they could never weary of it. The sun was high when they awoke the following morning. After breakfast, they held a consultation with respect to what was next to be done. From observation, Boone was satisfied that numbers of Indians, in small parties, were then in the neighborhood. He knew it was idle to suppose that two men, however brave and skilful in the use of their weapons, could survive long in opposition to them. He felt the impolicy of wasting more time in roaming over the country for the mere purpose of hunting.

He proposed to his brother that they should immediately set themselves seriously about selecting the most eligible spot on which permanently to fix his family. This done, they would return together to North Carolina to bring them out to the new country. He did not doubt, that he could induce a sufficient number to accompany him, to render a residence in it comparatively safe. That they might accomplish this purpose with as little delay as possible, they proceeded the remainder of the day to hunt, and prepare food sufficient for some time. The following day they completed the necessary arrangement, and settled every thing for departure on the next morning.

They directed their course to Cumberland river. In common with all explorers of unknown countries, they gave names to the streams which they crossed. After reaching Cumberland river, they traversed the region upon its banks in all directions for some days. Thence they took a more northern route, which led them to Kentucky river. The country around the latter river delighted them. Its soil and position were such as they sought; and they determined, that here should be the location of the new settlement. Having acquainted themselves, as far as they deemed necessary, with the character of the region to be revisited, their returning journey was recommenced. No incidents, but such as had marked all the period of their journeyings in the wilderness, the occasional encounter of Indians by day and the cries of wild beasts by night had happened to them, during their last exploration.

Upon the second day of their advance in the direction of their home, they heard the approach of a drove of buffaloes. The brothers remarked, that from the noise there must be an immense number, or some uncommon confusion among them. As the buffaloes came in view, the woodsmen saw the explanation of the unusual uproar in a moment. The herd were in a perfect fury, stamping the ground and tearing it up, and rushing back and forward upon one another in all directions. A panther had seated himself upon the back of one of the largest buffaloes, and fastened his claws and teeth into the flesh of the animal, wherever he could reach it, until the blood ran down on all sides. The movements of a powerful animal, under such suffering, may be imagined. But plunging, rearing, and running were to no purpose. The panther retained its seat, and continued its horrid work. The buffalo, in its agony, sought relief in the midst of its companions, but instead of obtaining it, communicated its fury to the drove.

The travellers did not care to approach the buffaloes too closely; but Boone, picking the flint of his rifle, and looking carefully at the loading, took aim at the panther, determined to displace the monster from its seat. It happened, that the buffalo continued a moment in a position to allow the discharge to take effect. The panther released its hold, and came to the ground. As generally happens in such cases, this herd was followed by a band of wolves. They prowl around for the remains usually found in the train of such numbers of animals. Another rifle was discharged among them, for the sport of seeing them scatter through the woods.

The brothers left such traces—or blazes as they are technically called—of their course, as they thought would enable them to find it again, until they reached the foot of the mountains. They tried various ascents, and finally discovered a route, which, with some labor might be rendered tolerably easy. They proposed to cross the families here, and blazed the path in a way that could not be mistaken. This important point settled, they hastened to the settlement, which they reached without accident.

CHAPTER VI.

Booue starts with his family to Kentucky—Their return to Clinch river—He conducts a party of surveyors to the Falls of Ohio—He helps build Boonesborough, and removes his family to the fort—His daughter and two of Col. Calloway's daughters taken prisoners by the Indians—They pursue the Indians and rescue the captives.

The next step was to collect a sufficient number of emigrants who would be willing to remove to the new country with the families of the Boones, to give the settlements security and strength to resist the attacks of the Indians. This was not an easy task. It may be readily imagined that the Boones saw only the bright side of the contemplated expedition. They painted the fertility and amenity of the flowering wilderness in the most glowing colors. They described the cane-brakes, the clover and grass, the transparent limestone springs and brooks, the open forests, the sugar maple orchards, the buffaloes, deer, turkeys and wild fowls, in all the fervid colors of their own imaginations. To them it was the paradise of the first pair, whose inhabitants had only to put forth their hands, and eat and enjoy. The depredations, captivities, and scalpings, of the Indians; the howling of the wolves; the diseases, and peculiar trials and difficulties of a new country, without houses, mills, and the most indispensable necessaries of civilized life, were all overlooked. But in such a case, in a compact settlement like that of the Yadkin, there are never wanting gainsayers, opposers, gossips, who envied the Boones.

These caused those disposed to the enterprise to hear the other part, and to contemplate the other side of the picture. They put stories in circulation as eloquent as those of the Boones, which told of all the scalpings, captivities, and murders of the Indians, magnified in a tenfold proportion. With them, the savages were like the ogres and bloody giants of nursery stories. They had pleasant tales of horn-snakes, of such deadly malignity, that the thorn in their tails, struck into the largest tree in full verdure, instantly blasted it. They scented in the air of the country, deadly diseases, and to them, Boone's paradise was a *Hinnom, the valley of the shadow of death.*

The minds of the half resolved, half doubting persons, that meditated emigration, vibrated alternately backwards and forwards, inclined or disinclined to it, according to the last view of the case presented to them. But the natural love of adventure, curiosity, fondness for the hunting life, dissatisfaction with the incessant labor necessary for subsistence on their present comparatively sterile soil, joined to the confident eloquence of the Boones, prevailed on four or five families to join them in the expedition.

All the necessary arrangements of preparing for this distant expedition, of making sales and purchases, had occupied nearly two years. The expedition commenced its march on the 26th of September, 1773. They all set forth with confident spirits for the western wilderness, and were joined by forty persons in Powell's Valley, a settlement in advance of that on the Yadkin, towards the western country. The whole made a cavalcade of nearly eighty persons.

The three principal ranges of the Alleghany, over which they must pass, were designated as Powell's, Walden's, and Cumberland. These mountains forming the barrier between the old settlements and the new country, stretch from the north-east to the south-west. They are of great length and breadth, and not far distant from each other. There are nature-formed passes over them, which render the ascent comparatively easy. The aspect of these huge piles was so wild and rugged, as to make it natural for those of the party who were unaccustomed to mountains, to express fears of being able to reach the opposite side. The course traced by the brothers on their return to Carolina, was found and followed. The advantage of this forethought was strongly perceived by all. Their progress was uninterrupted by any adverse circumstance, and every one was in high spirits, until the west side of Walden's ridge, the most elevated of the three, had been gained. They were now destined to experience a most appalling reverse of fortune.

On the tenth of October, as the party were advancing along a narrow defile, unapprehensive of danger, they were suddenly terrified by fearful yells. Instantly aware that Indians surrounded them, the men sprang to the defence of the helpless women and children. But the attack had been so sudden, and the Indians were so much superior in point of numbers, that six men fell at the first onset of the savages. A seventh was wounded, and the party would have been overpowered, but for a general and effective discharge of the rifles of the remainder. The Indians, terror-struck, took to flight, and disappeared.

Had the numbers of the travellers allowed it, they felt no inclination to pursue the retreating Indians. Their loss had been too serious to permit the immediate gratification of revenge. The eldest son of Daniel Boone was found among the slain. The domestic animals accompanying the expedition were so scattered by the noise of the affray, that it was impossible again to collect and recover them. The distress and discouragement of the party were so great, as to produce an immediate determination to drop the projected attempt of a settlement in Kentucky, and return to Clinch river, which lay forty miles in their rear, where a number of families had already fixed themselves.

They then proceeded to perform the last melancholy duties to the bodies of their unfortunate companions with all decent observances which circumstances would allow. Their return was then commenced. Boone and his brother, with some others, did not wish to forsake the undertaking upon which they had set out; but the majority against them was so great, and the feeling on the subject so strong, that they were compelled to acquiesce. The party retraced, in deep sadness, the steps they had so lately taken in cheerfulness, and even joy.

Daniel Boone remained with his family on Clinch river, until June. 1774; when he was requested by the governor of Virginia to go to the falls of Ohio, to act as a guide to a party of surveyors. The manifestations of hostility, on the part of the Indians, were such, that their longer stay was deemed unsafe. Boone undertook to perform this service, and set out upon this journey, with no other companion than a man by the name of Stoner. They reached the point of destination, now Louisville, in a surprisingly short period, without any accident. Under his guidance the surveyors arrived at the settlements in safety. From the time that Boone left his home, upon this enterprise, until he returned to it, was but sixty-two days. During this period he travelled eight hundred miles on foot, through a country entirely destitute of human habitations, save the camps of the Indians.

In the latter part of this year, the disturbances between the Indians north-west of the Ohio, and the frontier settlers, grew to open hostilities. Daniel Boone being in Virginia, the governor appointed him to the command of three contiguous garrisons on the frontier, with the commission of captain. The campaign of the year terminated in a battle, after which the militia were disbanded. Boone was consequently relieved from duty.

Col. Henderson, of North Carolina, had been for some time engaged in forming a company in that state, for the purpose of purchasing the lands on the south side of the Kentucky, from the southern Indians. The plan was now matured, and Boone was solicited by the company to attend the treaty to be made between them and the Indians, at Wataga, in March, 1775, to settle the terms of the negociation. The requisite information, in respect to the proposed purchase, was given him, and he acceded to the request. At the appointed time, he attended and successfully performed the service intrusted to him. Soon afterwards the same company applied to him to lay out a road between the settlements on Holston river and Kentucky river. No little knowledge of the country, and judgment were requisite for the proper fulfilment of this service. A great many different routes must be examined, before the most practicable one could be fixed upon. The duty was, however, executed by Boone, promptly and faithfully. The labor was great, owing to the rugged and mountainous country, through which the route led. The laborers, too, suffered from the repeated attacks of Indians. Four of them were killed, and five wounded. The remainder completed this work, by reaching Kentucky river, in April, of the same year. They immediately proceeded to erect a fort near a salt spring, where Boonesborough now stands. The party, enfeebled by its losses, did not complete the erection of the fort until June. The Indians troubled them exceedingly, and killed one man. The fort consisted of a block-house, and several cabins, surrounded by palisades.

The fort being finished, Boone returned to his family, and soon after removed them to this first garrison of Kentucky. The purpose on which his heart had so long been set, was now accomplished. His wife and daughters were the first white women that ever stood on the banks of Kentucky river. In our zeal to blazon our subject, it is not affirmed, that Boone was absolutely the first discoverer and explorer of Kentucky, for he was not. But the high meed of being the first actual settler and cultivator of the soil, cannot be denied him. It was the pleasant season of the close of summer and commencement of autumn, when the immigrants would see their new residence in the best light. Many of its actual inconveniences were withheld from observation, as the mildness of the air precluded the necessity of tight dwellings. Arrangements were made for cultivating a field in the coming spring. The Indians, although far from friendly, did not attempt any immediate assault upon their new neighbors, and the first events of the settlement were decidedly fortunate. The game in the woods was an unfailing resource for food. The supplies brought from their former homes by the immigrants were not yet exhausted, and things went on in their usual train, with the added advantage, that over all, in their new home, was spread the charm of novelty.

Winter came and passed with as little discomfort to the inmates of the garrison as could be expected from the circumstances of their position. The cabins were thoroughly daubed, and fuel was of course abundant. It is true, those who felled the trees were compelled to be constantly on their guard, lest a red man should take aim at them from the shelter of some one of the forest hiding places. But they were fitted for this way of getting along by their training, natures, and predilections. There was no want of excitement during the day, or even night—nothing of the wearying monotony to which a life of safe and regular occupation is subject. Spring opened. The trees were girdled, and the brush cut down and burned, preparatory to ploughing the field. A garden spot was marked off, the virgin earth thrown up and softened, and then given in charge to the wives and daughters of the establishment. They brought out their stock of seeds, gathered in the old settlements, and every bright day saw them engaged in the light and healthful occupation of planting them. They were protected by the vicinity of their husbands and fathers, and in turn cheered them in their severer labors. The Indians had forborne any attacks upon the settlers so long, that, as is naturally the case, they had ceased in a degree to dwell upon the danger always to be apprehended from them. The men did not fail to take their rifles and knives with them whenever they went abroad; but the women ventured occasionally a short distance without the palisades during the day, never, however, losing sight of the fort. This temerity was destined to cost them dear.

Colonel Calloway, the intimate friend of Boone, had joined him in the course of the spring, at the fort, which had received, by the consent of all, the name of Boonesborough. He had two daughters. Captain Boone had a daughter also, and the three were companions; and, if we may take the portraits of the rustic time, patterns of youthful bloom and loveliness. It cannot be doubted that they were inexpressibly dear to their parents. These girls, at the close of a beautiful summer day, the 14th of July, were tempted imprudently to wander into the woods at no great distance from their habitations, to gather flowers with which to adorn their rustic fire-places. They were suddenly surrounded by half a dozen Indians. Their shrieks and efforts to flee were alike unavailing. They were dragged rapidly beyond the power of making themselves heard. As soon as they were deemed to be beyond the danger of rescue, they were treated with the utmost indulgence and decorum.

This forbearance, of a race that we are accustomed to call savages, was by no means accidental, or peculiar to this case. While in battle, they are unsparing and unrelenting as tigers—while, after the fury of its excitement is past, they will exult with frantic and demoniac joy in the cries of their victims expiring at a slow fire—while they dash the tomahawk with merciless indifference into the cloven skulls of mothers and infants, they are universally seen to treat captive women with a decorous forbearance. This strange trait, so little in keeping with other parts of their character, has been attributed by some to their want of the sensibilities and passions of our race. The true solution is, the force of their habits. Honor, as they estimate it, is, with them, the most sacred and inviolable of all laws. The decorum of forbearance towards women in their power has been incorporated with their code as the peculiar honor of a warrior. It is usually kept sacred and inviolate. Instances are not wanting where they have shown themselves the most ardent lovers of their captives, and, we may add, most successful in gaining their voluntary affection in return. Enough such examples are recorded, were other proofs wanting, to redeem their forbearance from the negative character resulting from the want of passions.

The captors of these young ladies, having reached the main body of their people, about a dozen in number, made all the provision in their power for the comfort of their fair captives. They served them with their best provisions, and by signs and looks that could not be mistaken, attempted to soothe their agonies, and quiet their apprehensions and fears. The parents at the garrison, having waited in vain for the return of their gay and beloved daughters to prepare their supper, and in torments of suspense that may easily be imagined, until the evening, became aware that they were either lost or made captives. They sallied forth in search of them, and scoured the woods in every direction, without discovering a trace of them. They were then but too well convinced that they had been taken by the Indians. Captain Boone and Colonel Calloway, the agonizing parents of the lost ones, appealed to the company to obtain volunteers to pursue the Indians, under an oath, if they found the captors, either to retake their daughters, or die in the attempt. The oath of Boone on this occasion is recorded: "By the Eternal Power that made me a father, if my daughter lives, and is found, I will either bring her back, or spill my life blood." The oath was no sooner uttered than every individual of the males crowded round Boone to repeat it. But he reminded them that a part of their number must remain to defend the station. Seven select persons only were admitted to the oath, along with the fathers of the captives. The only difficulty was in making the selection. Supplying themselves with knapsacks, rifles, ammunition, and provisions, the party set forth on the pursuit.

Hitherto they had been unable to find the trail of the captors. Happily they fell upon it by accident. But the Indians, according to their custom, had taken so much precaution to hide their trail, that they found themselves exceedingly perplexed to keep it, and they were obliged to put forth all the acquirement and instinct of woodsmen not to find themselves every moment at fault in regard to their course. The rear Indians of the file had covered their foot prints with leaves. They often turned off at right angles; and whenever they came to a branch, walked in the water for some distance. At a place of this sort, the pursuers were for some time wholly unable to find at what point the Indians had left the branch, and began to despair of regaining their trail. In this extreme perplexity, one of the company was attracted by an indication of their course, which proved that the daughters shared the sylvan sagacity of their parents. "God bless my dear child," exclaimed Colonel Calloway; "she has proved that she had strength of mind in her deplorable condition to retain self-possession." At the same instant he picked up a little piece of ribbon, which he instantly recognized as his daughter's. She had evidently committed it unobserved to the air, to indicate the course of her captors. The trail was soon regained, and the company resumed their march with renewed alacrity.

They were afterwards often at a loss to keep the trail, from the extreme care of the Indians to cover and destroy it. But still, in their perplexity, the sagacious expedient of the fair young captives put them right. A shred of their handkerchief, or of some part of their dress, which they had intrusted to the wind unobserved, indicated their course, and that the captives were thus far not only alive, but that their reasoning powers, unsubdued by fatigue, were active and buoyant. Next day, in passing places covered with mud, deposited by the dry branches on the way, the foot prints of the captives were distinctly traced, until the pursuers had learned to discriminate not only the number, but the peculiar form of each foot print.

Late in the evening of the fifteenth day's pursuit, from a little eminence, they discovered in the distance before them, through the woods, a smoke and the light of a fire. The palpitation of their parental hearts may be easily imagined. They could not doubt that it was the camp of the captors of their children. The plan of recapture was intrusted entirely to Boone. He led his company as near the enemy as he deemed might be done with safety, and selecting a position under the shelter of a hill, ordered them to halt, with a view to passing the night in that place. They then silently took food as the agitation of their minds would allow. All but Calloway, another selected person of their number, and himself, were permitted to lie down, and get that sleep of which they had been so long deprived. The three impatiently waited for midnight, when the sleep of the Indians would be most likely to be profound. They stationed the third person selected, on the top of the eminence, behind which they were encamped, as a sentinel to await a given signal from the fathers, which should be his indication to fly to the camp and arouse the sleepers, and bring them to their aid. Then falling prostrate, they crept cautiously, and as it were by inches, towards the Indian camp.

Having reached a covert of bushes, close by the Indian camp, and examined as well as they could by the distant light of the camp-fires, the order of their rifles, they began to push aside the bushes, and survey the camp through the opening. Seventeen Indians were stretched, apparently in sound sleep, on the ground. But they looked in vain among them for the dear objects of their pursuit. They were not long in discovering another camp a little remote from that of the Indians. They crawled cautiously round to take a survey of it. Here, to their inexpressible joy, were their daughters in each others arms. Directly in front of their camp were two Indians, with their tomahawks and other weapons within their grasp. The one appeared to be in a sound sleep, and the other keeping the most circumspective vigils.

The grand object now was to get possession of the

prisoners without arousing their captors, the consequence of which it was obvious, would be the immediate destruction of the captives. Boone made a signal to Calloway to take a sure aim at the sleeping Indian, so as to be able to despatch him in a moment, if the emergency rendered that expedient necessary. Boone, the while, crawled round, so as to reach the waking Indian from behind; intending to spring upon him and strangle him, so as to prevent his making a noise to awaken the sleeper. But, unfortunately, this Indian instead of being asleep was wide awake, and on a careful look out. The shadow of Boone coming on them from behind, aroused him. He sprang erect, and uttered a yell that made the ancient woods ring, leaving no doubt that the other camp would be instantly alarmed. The captives, terrified by the war yell of their sentinels, added their screams of apprehension, and every thing was in a moment in confusion. The first movement of Boone was to fire. But the forbearance of Calloway, and his own more prudent second thought, restrained him. It was hard to forego such a chance for vengeance, but their own lives and their children's would probably pay the forfeit, and they fired not. On the contrary, they surrendered themselves to the Indians, who rushed furiously in a mass around them. By significant gestures, and a few Indian words, which they had learned, they implored the lives of their captive children, and opportunity for a parley. Seeing them in their power, and comprehending the language of defenceless suppliants, their fury was at length with some difficulty restrained and appeased. They seemed evidently under the influence of a feeling of compassion towards the daughters, to which unquestionably the adventurous fathers were indebted, that their lives were not instantly sacrificed. Binding them firmly with cords, and surrounding them with sentinels, the Indians retired to their camp, not to resume their sleep, but to hold a council to settle the fate of their new prisoners.

What were the thoughts of the captive children, or of the disinterested and brave parents, as they found themselves bound, and once more in the power of their enemies—what was the bitter disappointment of the one, and the agonizing filial apprehension of the other—may be much more readily imagined than described. But the light of the dawn enabled the daughters to see, in the countenances of their fathers, as they lay bound and surrounded by fierce savages, unextinguishable firmness, and undaunted resolution, and a consciousness of noble motives; and they imbibed from the view something of the magnanimity of their parents, and assumed that demeanor of composure and resolute endurance which is always the readiest expedient to gain all the respect and forbearance that an Indian can grant.

It would be difficult to fancy a state of more torturing suspense than that endured by the companions of Boone and Calloway, who had been left behind the hill. Though they had slept little since the commencement of the expedition, and had been encouraged by the two fathers, their leaders to sleep that night, the emergency was too exciting to admit of sleep.

Often, during the night, had they aroused themselves, in expectation of the return of the fathers, or of a signal for action. But the night wore away, and the morning dawned, without bringing either the one or the other. But notwithstanding this distressing state of suspense, they had a confidence too undoubting in the firmness and prudence of their leader, to think of approaching the Indian camp until they should receive the appointed signal.

It would naturally be supposed that the deliberation of the Indian council, which had been held to settle the fate of Boone and Calloway, would end in sentencing them to run the gauntlet, and then amidst the brutal laughter and derision of their captors, to be burnt to death at a slow fire. Had the prisoners betrayed the least signs of fear, the least indications of a subdued mind, such would in all probability have been the issue of the Indian consultation. Such, however, was not the result of the council. It was decreed that they should be killed with as little noise as possible; their scalps taken as trophies, and that their daughters should remain captives as before. The lenity of this sentence may be traced to two causes. The daring hardihood, the fearless intrepidity of the adventure, inspired them with unqualified admiration for their captives. Innumerable instances have since been recorded, where the most inveterate enemies have boldly ventured into the camp of their enemy, have put themselves in their power, defied them to their face and have created an admiration of their fearless daring, which has caused that they have been spared and dismissed unmolested. This sort of feeling had its influence on the present occasion in favor of the prisoners. Another extenuating influence was, that hostilities between the white and red men in the west had as yet been uncommon; and the mutual fury had not been exasperated by murder and retaliation.

As soon as it was clear morning light, the Indian camp was in motion. As a business preliminary to their march, Boone and Calloway were led out and bound to a tree, and the warriors were selected who were to despatch them with their tomahawks. The place of their execution was selected at such a distance from their camp, as that the daughters might not be able to witness it. The two prisoners were already at the spot, awaiting the fatal blow, when a discharge of rifles, cutting down two of the savages at the first shot, arrested their proceedings. Another and another discharge followed. The Indians were as yet partially supplied with fire arms, and had not lost any of their original dread of the effects of this artificial thunder, and the invisible death of the balls. They were ignorant, moreover, of the number of their assailants, and naturally apprehended it to be greater than it was. They raised a yell of confusion, and dispersed in every direction, leaving their dead behind, and the captives to their deliverers. The next moment the children were in the arms of their parents; and the whole party, in the unutterable joy of con-

quest and deliverance, were on their way homewards.

It need hardly be added that the brave associates of the expedition who had been left in camp, having waited the signal for the return of Boone and Calloway, until their patience and forbearance was exhausted, aware that something serious must have prevented their return, reconnoitered the movement of the Indians as they moved from their camp to despatch their two prisoners, and fired upon them at the moment they were about to put their sentence into execution.

About this time a new element began to exasperate and extend the ravages of Indian warfare, along the whole line of the frontier settlements. The war of Independence had already begun to rage. The influence and resources of Great Britain extended along the immense chain of our frontier, from the north-eastern part of Vermont and New York, all the way to the Mississippi. Nor did this nation, to her everlasting infamy, hesitate to engage these infuriate allies of the wilderness, whose known rule of warfare was indiscriminate vengeance, without reference to the age or sex of the foe, as auxiliaries in the war.

As this biographical sketch of the life of Boone is inseparably interwoven with this border scene of massacres, plunderings, burnings, and captivities, which swept the incipient northern and western settlements with desolation, it may not be amiss to take a brief retrospect of the state of these settlements at this conjuncture in the life of Boone.

CHAPTER VII.

Settlement of Harrodsburgh—Indian mode of besieging and warfare—Fortitude and privation of the Pioneers—The Indians attack Harrodsburgh and Boonesborough—Description of a Station—Attack of Bryant's Station.

A ROAD sufficient for the passage of pack horses in single file, had been opened from the settlements already commenced on Holston river to Boonesborough in Kentucky. It was an avenue which soon brought other adventurers, with their families to the settlement. On the northern frontier of the country, the broad and unbroken bosom of the Ohio opened an easy liquid highway of access to the country. The first spots selected as landing places and points of ingress into the country, were Limestone—now Maysville—at the mouth of Limestone creek, and Beargrass creek, where Louisville now stands. Boonesborough and Harrodsburgh were the only stations in Kentucky sufficiently strong to be safe from the incursions of the Indians; and even these places afforded no security a foot beyond the palisades. These two places were the central points towards which emigrants directed their course from Limestone and Louisville. The routes from these two places were often ambushed by the Indians. But notwithstanding the danger of approach to the new country, and the incessant exposure during the residence there, immigrants continued to arrive at the stations.

The first female white settlers of Harrodsburgh, were Mrs. Denton, McGary, and Hogan, who came with their husbands and families. A number of other families soon followed, among whom, in 1776, came Benjamin Logan, with his wife and family. These were all families of respectability and standing, and noted in the subsequent history of the country.

Hordes of savages were soon afterwards ascertained to have crossed the Ohio, with the purpose to extirpate these germs of social establishments in Kentucky. According to their usual mode of warfare, they separated into numerous detachments, and dispersed in all directions through the forests. This gave them the aspect of numbers and strength beyond reality. It tended to increase the apprehensions of the recent immigrants, inspiring the natural impressions, that the woods in all directions were full of Indians. It enabled them to fight in detail,—to assail different settlements at the same time, and to fill the whole country with consternation.

Their mode of besieging these places, though not at all conformable to the notions of a siege derived from the tactics of a civilized people, was dictated by the most profound practical observation, operating upon existing circumstances. Without cannon or scaling ladders, their hope of carrying a station, or fortified place, was founded upon starving the inmates, cutting off their supplies of water, killing them, as they exposed themselves, in detail, or getting possession of the station by some of the arts of dissimulation. Caution in their tactics is still more strongly inculcated than bravery. Their first object is to secure themselves; their next, to kill their enemy. This is the universal Indian maxim from Nova Zembla to Cape Horn. In besieging a place, they are seldom seen in force upon any particular quarter. Acting in small parties, they disperse themselves, and lie concealed among bushes or weeds, behind trees or stumps. They ambush the paths to the barn, spring, or field. They discharge their rifle or let fly their arrow, and glide away without being seen, content that their revenge should issue from an invisible source. They kill the cattle, watch the watering places, and cut off all supplies. During the night, they creep, with the inaudible and stealthy step dictated by the animal instinct, to a concealed position near one of the gates, and patiently pass many sleepless nights, so that they may finally cut off some ill-fated person, who incautiously comes forth in the morning. During the day, if there be near the station grass, weeds, bushes, or any distinct elevation of the soil, however small, they crawl, as prone as reptiles, to the place of concealment, and whoever exposes the smallest part of his body through any part or chasm, receives their shot, behind the smoke of which they instantly cower back to their retreat. When they find their foe abroad, they boldly rush upon him, and make him prisoner, or take his scalp. At times they approach the walls or palisades with the most audacious daring, and attempt to fire them, or beat down the gate. They practice, with the utmost adroitness, the stratagem of a false alarm on one side when the real assault is intended for the other. With untiring perseverance, when their stock of provisions is exhausted, they set forth to hunt, as on common occasions, resuming their station near the beseiged place as soon as they are supplied.

It must be confessed, that they had many motives to this persevering and deadly hostility, apart from their natural propensity to war. They saw this new and hated race of pale faces gradually getting possession of their hunting grounds, and cutting down their forests. They reasoned forcibly and justly, that the time, when to oppose these new intruders with success, was to do it before they had become numerous and strong in diffused population and resources. Had they possessed the skill of corporate union, combining individual effort with a general concert of attack, and directed their united force against each settlement in succession, there is little doubt, that at this time they might have extirpated the new inhabitants from Kentucky, and have restored it to the empire of the wild beasts and the red men. But in the order of events it was otherwise arranged. They massacred, they burnt, and plundered, and destroyed. They killed cattle, and carried off the horses;—inflicting terror, poverty, and every species of distress; but were not able to make themselves absolute masters of a single station.

It has been found by experiment, that the settlers in such predicaments of danger and apprehension, act under a most spirit-stirring excitement, which, notwithstanding its alarms, is not without its pleasures. They acquired fortitude, dexterity, and that kind of courage which results from becoming familiar with exposure.

The settlements becoming extended, the Indians, in their turn, were obliged to put themselves on the defensive. They cowered in the distant woods for concealment, or resorted to them for hunting. In these intervals, the settlers, who had acquired a kind of instinctive intuition to know when their foe was near them, or had retired to remoter forests, went forth to plough their corn, gather in their harvests, collect their cattle, and pursue their agricultural operations. These were their holyday seasons for hunting, during which they often exchanged shots with their foe. The night, as being most secure from Indian attack, was the common season selected for journeying from garrison to garrison.

We, who live in the midst of scenes of abundance and tranquillity can hardly imagine how a country could fill with inhabitants, under so many circumstances of terror, in addition to all the hardships incident to the commencement of new establishments in the wilderness; such as want of society, want of all the regular modes of supply, in regard to the articles most indispensable in every stage of the civilized condition. There were no mills, no stores, no regular supplies of clothing, salt, sugar, and the luxuries of tea and coffee. But all these dangers and difficulties notwithstanding, under the influence of an inexplicable propensity, families in the old settlements used to comfort and abundance, were constantly arriving to encounter all these dangers and privations. They began to spread over the extensive and fertile country in every direction —presenting such numerous and dispersed marks to Indian hostility, red men became perplexed, amidst so many conflicting temptations to vengeance, which to select.

The year 1776 was memorable in the annals of Kentucky, as that in which General George Rogers Clark first visited it, unconscious, it may be, of the imperishable honors which the western country would one day reserve for him. This same year, Captain Wagin arrived in the country, and *fixed* in a solitary cabin on Hinkston's Fork of the Licking.

In the autumn of this year, most of the recent immigrants to Kentucky returned to the old settlements, principally in Virginia. They carried with them strong representations, touching the fertility and advantages of their new residence; and communicated the impulse of their hopes and fears extensively among their fellow-citizens by sympathy.

The importance of the new settlement was already deemed to be such, that on the meeting of the legislature of Virginia, the governor recommended that the south-western part of the county of Fincastle— so this vast tract of country west of the Alleghanies had hitherto been considered—should be erected into a separate county by the name of Kentucky.

This must be considered an important era in the history of the country. The new county became entitled to two representatives in the legislature of Virginia, to a court and judge; in a word, to all the customary civil, military, and judicial officers of a new county. In the year 1777, the county was duly organized, according to the act of the Virginia legislature. Among the names of the first officers in the new county, we recognize those of Floyd, Bowman, Logan, and Todd.

Harrodsburgh, the strongest and most populous station in the country, had not hitherto been assailed by the Indians. Early in the spring of 1777, they attacked a small body of improvers marching to Harrodsburgh, about four miles from that place. Mr. Kay, afterwards General Kay, and his brother were of the party. The latter was killed, and another man made prisoner. The fortunate escape of James Kay, then fifteen years old, was the probable cause of the saving of Harrodsburgh from destruction. Flying from the scene of attack and the death of his brother, he reached the station and gave the inhabitants information, that a large body of Indians was marching to attack the place. The Indians themselves, aware that the inhabitants had been premonished of their approach, seem to have been disheartened; for they did not reach the station till the next day. Of course, it had been put in the best possible state of defence, and prepared for their reception.

The town was now invested by the savage force, and something like a regular siege commenced. A brisk firing ensued. In the course of the day the Indians left one of their dead to fall into the hands of the besieged—a rare occurrence, as it is one of their most invariable customs to remove their wounded and dead from the possession of the enemy. The besieged had four men wounded and one of them mortally. The Indians, unacquainted with the mode of conducting a siege, and little accustomed to open and fair fight, and dispirited by the vigorous reception given them by the station, soon decamped, and dispersed in the forests, to supply themselves with provisions by huntıng.

On the 15th of April, 1777, a body of one hundred savages invested Boonesborough, the residence of Daniel Boone. The greater number of the Indians had fire arms, though some of them were still armed with bows and arrows. This station, having its defence conducted by such a gallant leader, gave them such a warm reception that they were glad to draw off; though not till they had killed one and wounded four of the inhabitants. Their loss could not be ascertained, as they carefully removed their dead and wounded.

In July following, the residence of Boone was again besieged by a body of Indians, whose number was increased to two hundred. With their numbers, their hardihood and audacity were increased in proportion. To prevent the neighboring stations from sending assistance, detachments from their body assailed most of the adjacent settlements at the same time. The gallant inmates of the station made them repent their temerity, though, as formerly, with some loss; one of their number having been killed and two wounded. Seven of the Indians were distinctly counted from the fort among the slain; though, according to custom, the bodies were removed. After a close siege, and almost constant firing during two days, the Indians raised a yell of disappointment, and disappeared in the forests.

In order to present distinct views of the sort of enemy, with whom Boone had to do, and to present pictures of the aspect of Indian warfare in those times, we might give sketches of the repeated sieges of Harrodsburgh and Boonesborough, against which —as deemed the strong holds of the *Long-knife*, as they called the Americans—their most formidable and repeated efforts were directed. There is such a sad and dreary uniformity in these narratives, that the history of one may almost stand for that of all. They always present more or less killed and wounded on the part of the stations, and a still greater number on that of the Indians. Their attacks of stations having been uniformly unsuccessful, they returned to their original modes of warfare, dispersing themselves in small bodies over all the country, and attacking individual settlers in insulated cabins, and destroying women and children. But as most of these annals belong to the general history of Kentucky, and do not particularly tend to develop the character of the subject of this biography, we shall pretermit them, with a single exception. At the expense of an anachronism, and as a fair sample of the rest, we shall present that, as one of the most prominent Indian sieges recorded in these early annals. It will not be considered an episode, if it tend to convey distinct ideas of the structure and form of a *station*, and the modes of attack and defence in those times. It was in such scenes that the fearless daring, united with the cool, prudent, and yet efficient counsels of Daniel Boone, were peculiarly conspicuous. With this view we offer a somewhat detailed account of the attack of Bryant's station.

As we know of no place, nearer than the sources of the Mississippi, or the Rocky Mountains, where the refuge of a *station* is now requisite for security from the Indians; as the remains of those that were formerly built are fast mouldering to decay; and as in a few years history will be the only depository of what the term *station* imports, we deem it right, in this place, to present as graphic a view as we may, of a station, as we have seen them in their ruins in various points of the west.

The first immigrants to Tennessee and Kentucky, as we have seen, came in pairs and small bodies. These pioneers on their return to the old settlements, brought back companies and societies.—Friends and connections, old and young, mothers and daughters, flocks, herds, domestic animals, and the family dogs, all set forth on the patriarchal emigration for the land of promise together. No disruption of the tender natal and moral ties; no annihilation of the reciprocity of domestic kindness, friendship, and love, took place. The cement and and panoply of affection, and good will bound them together at once in the social tie, and the union for defence. Like the gregarious tenants of the air in their annual migrations, they brought their true home, that is to say their charities with them. In their state of extreme isolation from the world they had left, the kindly social propensities were found to grow more strong in the wilderness. The current of human affections in fact naturally flows in a deeper and more vigorous tide, in proportion as it is diverted into fewer channels.

These immigrants to the Bloody Ground, coming to survey new aspects of nature, new forests and climates, and to encounter new privations, difficulties and dangers, were bound together by a new sacrament of friendship, new and unsworn oaths, to stand by each other for life and for death. How often have we heard the remains of this primitive race of Kentucky deplore the measured distance and jealousy, the heathen rivalry and selfishness of the present generation, in comparison with the unity of heart, dangers and fortunes of these primeval times—reminding one of the simple kindness, the community of property, and the union of heart among the first Christians!

Another circumstance of this picture ought to be redeemed from oblivion. We suspect that the general impressions of the readers of this day is, that the first hunters and settlers of Kentucky and Tennessee were a sort of demi-savages. Imagination depicts them with long beard, and a costume of skins, rude, fierce, and repulsive. Nothing can be wider from the fact. These progenitors of the west were generally men of noble, square, erect forms, broad chests, clear, bright, truth-telling eyes, and of vigorous intellects.

All this is not only matter of historical record, but in the natural order of things. The first settlers of America were originally a noble stock. These, their descendants, had been reared under circumstances every way calculated to give them manly beauty and noble forms. They had breathed a free and a salubrious air. The field and forest exercise yielded them salutary viands, and appetite and digestion corresponding. Life brought them the sensations of high health, herculean vigor, and redundant joy.

When a social band of this description had planted their feet on the virgin soil, the first object was to fix on a spot, central to the most fertile tract of land that could be found, combining the advantages usually sought by the first settlers. Among these was, that the station should be on the summit of a gentle swell, where pawpaw, cane, and wild clover, marked exuberant fertility; and where the trees were so sparse, and the soil beneath them so free from underbrush, that the hunter could ride at half speed. The virgin soil, as yet friable, untrodden, and not cursed with the blight of politics, party, and feud, yielded, with little other cultivation than planting, from eighty to a hundred bushels of maize to the acre, and all other edibles suited to the soil and climate, in proportion.

The next thing, after finding this central nucleus of a settlement, was to convert it into a *station*, an erection which now remains to be described. It was a desirable requisite, that a station should inclose or command a flush limestone spring, for water for the settlement. The contiguity of a salt lick and a sugar orchard, though not indispensable, was a very desirable circumstance. The next preliminary step was to clear a considerable area, so as to leave nothing within a considerable distance of the station that could shelter an enemy from observation and a shot. If a spring were not inclosed, or a well dug within, as an Indian siege seldom lasted beyond a few days, it was customary, in periods of alarm to have a reservoir of some sort within the station, that should be filled with water enough to supply the garrison, during the probable continuance of a siege. It was deemed a most important consideration, that the station should overlook and command as much of the surrounding country as possible.

The form was a perfect parallelogram, including from a half to a whole acre. A trench was then dug four or five feet deep, and large and contiguous pickets planted in this trench, so as to form a compact wall from ten to twelve feet high above the soil. The pickets were of hard and durable timber, about a foot in diameter. The soil about them was rammed hard. They formed a rampart beyond the power of man to leap, climb, or by unaided physical strength to overthrow. At the angles were small projecting squares, of still stronger material and planting, technically called *flankers*, with oblique port-holes, so as that the sentinel within could rake the extetnal front of the station, without being exposed to shot from without. Two folding gates in the front and rear, swinging on prodigious wooden hinges, gave egress and ingress to men and teams in times of security.

In periods of alarm a trusty sentinel on the roof of the building was so stationed, as to be able to descry every suspicious object while yet in the distance. The gates were always firmly barred by night; and sentinels took their alternate watch, and relieved each other until morning. Nothing in the line of fortification can be imagined more easy of construction, or a more effectual protection against a savage enemy, than this simple erection. Though the balls of the smallest dimensions of cannon would have swept them away with ease, they were proof against the Indian rifle, patience, and skill. The only expedient of the red men was to dig under them and undermine them, or destroy them by fire; and even this could not be done without exposing them to the rifles of the flankers. Of course, there are few recorded instances of their having been taken, when defended by a garrison, guided by such men as Daniel Boone.

Their regular form, and their show of security, rendered these walled cities in the central wilderness delightful spectacles in the eye of immigrants who had come two hundred leagues without seeing a human habitation. Around the interior of these walls the habitations of the immigrants arose, and the remainder of the surface was a clean-turfed area for wrestling and dancing, and the vigorous and athletic amusements of the olden time. It is questionable if heartier dinners and profounder sleep, and more exhilarating balls and parties fall to the lot of their descendants, who ride in coaches and dwell in mansions. Venison and wild turkeys, sweet potatoes and pies, smoked on their table; and persimmon and maple beer, stood them well instead of the poisonous whisky of their children.

The community, of course, passed their social evenings together; and while the fire blazed bright within the secure square, the far howl of wolves, or even the distant war-whoop of the savages, sounded in the ear of the tranquil in-dwellers like the driving storm pouring on the sheltering roof above the head of the traveller safely reposing in his bed; that is, brought the contrast of comfort and security with more home-felt influence to their bosom.

Such a station was Bryant's, no longer ago than 1782. It was the nucleus of the settlements of that rich and delightful country, of which at present Lexington is the centre. There were but two others of any importance, at this time north of Kentucky river. It was more open to attack than any other in the country. The Miami on the north, and the Licking on the south of the Ohio, were long canals, which floated the Indian canoes from the northern hive of the savages, between the lakes and the Ohio, directly to its vicinity.

In the summer of this year a grand Indian assemblage took place at Chillicothe, a famous central Indian town on the Little Miami. The Cherokees, Wyandots, Tawas, Pottawattomies, and most of the tribes bordering on the lakes, were represented in it. Besides their chiefs and some Canadians, they were aided by the counsels of the two Girtys, and McKee, renegado whites. We have made diligent enquiry touching the biography of these men, particularly Simon Girty, a wretch of most infamous notoriety in those times, as a more successful instigator of Indian assault and massacre, than any name on record. Scarcely a tortured captive escaped from the northern Indians, who could not tell the share which this villain had in his sufferings—no burning or murder of prisoners, at which he had not assisted by his presence or his counsels. These refugees from our white settlements, added the calculation and power of combining of the whites to the instinctive cunning and ferocity of the savages. They possessed their thirst for blood without their active or passive courage—blending the bad points of character in the whites and Indians, without the good of either. The cruelty of the Indians had some show of palliating circumstances, in the steady encroachments of the whites upon them. Theirs was gratuitous, cold-blooded, and without visible motive, except that they appeared to hate the race more inveterately for having fled from it. Yet Simon Girty, like the Indians among whom he lived, sometimes took the freak of kindness, nobody could divine why, and he once or twice saved an unhappy captive from being roasted alive.

This vile renegado, consulted by the Indians as an oracle, lived in plenty, smoked his pipe, and drank off his whisky in his log palace. He was seen abroad clad in a ruffled shirt, a red and blue uniform, with pantaloons and gaiters to match. He was belted with dirks and pistols, and wore a watch with enormous length of chain, and most glaring ornaments, all probably the spoils of murder. So habited, he strutted, in the enormity of his cruelty in view of the ill-fated captives of the Indians, like the peacock spreading his morning plumage. There is little doubt that his capricious acts of saving the few that were spared through his intercession, were modified results of vanity; and that they were spared to make a display of his power, and the extent of his influence among the Indians.

The assemblage of Indians bound to the assault of Bryant's station, gathered round the shrine of Simon Girty, to hear the response of this oracle touching the intended expedition. He is said to have painted to them, in a set speech, the abundance and delight of the fair valleys of Kan-tuck-ee, for which so much blood of red men had been shed—the land of clover, deer, and buffaloes. He described the gradual encroachment of the whites, and the certainty that they would soon occupy the whole land. He proved the necessity of a vigorous, united, and persevering effort against them, now while they were feeble, and had scarcely gained foot-hold on the soil, if they ever intended to regain possession of their ancient, rich, and rightful domain; assuring them, that as things now went on, they would soon have no hunting grounds worth retaining, no blankets with which to clothe their naked backs, or whisky to warm and cheer their desolate hearts. They were advised to descend the Miami, cross the Ohio. ascend the Licking, paddling their canoes to the immediate vicinity of Bryant's station, which he counselled them to attack.

Forthwith, the mass of biped wolves raised their murderous yell, as they started for their canoes on the Miami. Girty, in his ruffled shirt and soldier coat, stalked at their head. silently feeding upon his prowess and grandeur.

The station against which they were destined, inclosed forty cabins. They arrived before it on the fifteenth of August, in the night. The inhabitants were advertised of their arrival in the morning, by being fired upon as they opened the gates. The time of their arrival was apparently providential. In two hours most of the efficient male inmates of the station were to have marched to the aid of two other stations, which were reported to have been attacked. This place would thus have been left completely defenceless. As soon as the garrison saw themselves besieged, they found means to despatch one of their number to Lexington, to announce the assault and crave aid. Sixteen mounted men, and thirty-one on foot, were immediately despatched to their assistance.

The number of the assailants amounted to at least six hundred. In conformity with the common modes of their warfare, they attempted to gain the place by stratagem. The great body concealed themselves among high weeds, on the opposite side of the station, within pistol shot of the spring which supplied it with water. A detachment of a hundred commenced a false attack on the south-east angle, with a view to draw the whole attention of the garrison to that point. They hoped that while the chief force of the station crowded there, the opposite point would be left defenceless. In this instance they reckoned without their host. The people penetrated their deception, and instead of returning their fire, commenced what had been imprudently neglected, the repairing their palisades, and putting the station in a better condition of defence. The tall and luxuriant strammony weeds instructed these wary backwoodsmen to suspect that a host of their tawny foe lay hid beneath their sheltering foliage, lurking for a chance to fire upon them, as they should come forth for water.

Let modern wives, who refuse to follow their husbands abroad, alleging the danger of the voyage or journey, or the unhealthiness of the proposed residence, or because the removal will separate them from the pleasures of fashion and society, contemplate the example of the wives of the defenders of this station. These noble mothers, wives, and daughters, assuring the men that there was no probability that the Indians would fire upon them, offered to go out and draw water for the supply of the garrison, and that even if they did shoot down a few of them, it would not reduce the resources of the garrison as would the killing of the men. The illustrious heroines took up their buckets, and marched out to the spring, espying here and there a painted face, or an Indian body crouched under the covert of the weeds. Whether their courage or their beauty fascinated the Indians to suspend their fire, does not appear. But it was so, that these generous women came and went until the reservoir was amply supplied with water. Who will doubt that the husbands of such wives must have been alike gallant and affectionate?

After this example, it was not difficult to procure

some young volunteers to tempt the Indians in the same way. As was expected, they had scarcely advanced beyond their station, before a hundred Indians fired a shower of balls upon them, happily too remote to do more than inflict slight wounds with spent balls. They retreated within the palisades, and the whole Indian force, seeing no results from stratagem, rose from their covert and rushed towards the palisade. The exasperation of their rage may be imagined, when they found every thing prepared for their reception. A well aimed fire drove them to a more cautious distance. Some of the more audacious of their number, however, ventured so near a less exposed point, as to be able to discharge burning arrows upon the roofs of the houses. Some of them were fired and burnt. But an easterly wind providentially arose at the moment, and secured the mass of the habitations from the further spread of the flames. These they could no longer reach with their burning arrows.

The enemy cowered back, and crouched to their covert in the weeds; where, panther-like, they waited for less dangerous game. They had divided, on being informed, that aid was expected from Lexington; and they arranged an ambuscade to intercept it, on its approach to the garrison. When the reinforcement, consisting of forty-six persons, came in sight, the firing had wholly ceased, and the invisible enemy were profoundly still. The auxiliaries hurried on in reckless confidence, under the impression that they had come on a false alarm. A lane opened an avenue to the station, through a thick cornfield.

This lane was way-laid on either side, by Indians, for six hundred yards. Fortunately, it was mid-summer, and dry; and the horsemen raised so thick a cloud of dust, that the Indians could fire only at random amidst the palpable cloud, and happily killed not a single man. The footmen were less fortunate. Being behind the horse, as soon as they heard the firing, they dispersed into the thick corn, in hopes to reach the garrison unobserved. They were intercepted by masses of the savages, who threw themselves between them and the station. Hard fighting ensued, in which two of the footmen were killed and four wounded. Soon after the detachment had joined their friends, and the Indians were again crouching close in their covert, the numerous flocks and herds of the station came in from the woods as usual, quietly ruminating, as they made their way towards their night-pens. Upon these harmless animals the Indians wreaked unmolested revenge, and completely destroyed them.

A little after sunset the famous Simon, in all his official splendor, covertly approached the garrison, mounted a stump, whence he could be heard by the people of the station, and holding a flag of truce, demanded a parley and the surrender of the place. He managed his proposals with no small degree of art, assigning, in imitation of the commanders of what are called civilized armies, that his proposals were dictated by humanity and a wish to spare the effusion of blood. He affirmed, that in case of a prompt surrender, he could answer for the safety of the prisoners; but that in the event of taking the garrison by storm, he could not; that cannon and a reinforcement were approaching, in which case they must be aware that their palisades could no longer interpose any resistance to their attack, or secure them from the vengeance of an exasperated foe. He calculated that his imposing language would have the more effect in producing belief and consternation, inasmuch as the garrison must know, that the same foe had used cannon in the attack of Ruddle's and Martin's stations. Two of their number had been already slain, and there were four wounded in the garrison; and some faces were seen to blanch as Girty continued his harangue of menace, and insidious play upon their fears. Some of the more considerate of the garrison, apprised by the result, of the folly of allowing such a negotiation to intimidate the garrison in that way, called out to shoot the rascal, adding the customary Kentucky epithet. Girty insisted upon the universal protection every where accorded to a flag of truce, while this parley lasted; and demanded with great assumed dignity, if they did not know who it was that thus addressed them?

A spirited young man, named Reynolds, of whom the most honorable mention is made in the subsequent annals of the contests with the Indians, was selected by the garrison to reply to the renegado Indian negotiator. His object seems to have been to remove the depression occasioned by Girty's speech, by treating it with derision; and perhaps to establish a reputation for successful waggery, as he had already for hard fighting.

"You ask," answered he, "if we do not know you?

Know you! Yes. We know you too well. Know Simon Girty! Yes. He is the renegado, cowardly villain, who loves to murder women and children, especially those of his own people. Know Simon Girty! Yes. His father was a panther and his dam a wolf. I have a worthless dog, that kills lambs. Instead of shooting him, I have named him Simon Girty. You expect reinforcements and cannon, do you? Cowardly wretches, like you, that make war upon women and children, would not dare to touch them off, if you had them. We expect reinforcements, too, and in numbers to give a short account of the murdering cowards that follow you. Even if you could batter down our pickets, I, for one, hold your people in too much contempt to discharge rifles at them. Should you see cause to enter our fort, I have been roasting a great number of hickory switches, with which we mean to whip your naked cut-throats out of the country."

Simon, apparently little edified or flattered by this speech, wished him some of his hardest curses; and affecting to deplore the obstinacy and infatuation of the garrison, the ambassador of ruffled shirt and soldier coat withdrew. The besieged gave a good account of every one, who came near enough to take a fair shot. But before morning they decamped, marching direct to the Blue Licks, where they obtained very different success, and a most signal and bloody triumph. We shall there again meet Daniel Boone, in his accustomed traits of heroism and magnanimity.

CHAPTER VIII.

Boone being attacked by two Indians near the Blue Licks, kills them both—Is afterwards taken prisoner and marched to Old Chillicothe—Is adopted by the Indians—Indian ceremonies.

We return to the subject of our memoir, from which the reader may imagine we have wandered too long. He had already conducted the defence of Boonesborough, during two Indian sieges. The general estimate of his activity, vigilance, courage, and enterprise, was constantly rising. By the Indians he was regarded as the most formidable and intelligent captain of the Long-knife; and by the settlers and immigrants as a disinterested and heroic patriarch of the infant settlements. He often supplied destitute families gratuitously with game. He performed the duties of surveyor and spy, generally as a volunteer, and without compensation. When immigrant families were approaching the country, he often went out to meet them and conduct them to the settlements. Such, in general, were the paternal feelings of the pioneers of this young colony.

The country was easily and amply supplied with meat from the chase, and with vegetables from the fertility of the soil. The hardy settlers could train themselves without difficulty to dispense with many things which habit and long use in the old settlements had led them to consider as necessaries. But to every form of civilized communities salt is an indispensable article. The settlement of Boonesborough had been fixed near a lick, with a view to the supply of that article. But the amount was found to be very inadequate to the growing demand. The settlement deemed it necessary to send out a company to select a place where the whole country could be supplied with that article at a reasonable rate.

Captain Boone was deputed by the settlers to this service. He selected thirty associates, and set out on the first of January, 1779, for the Blue Licks, on Licking river, a well known stream emptying into the Ohio, opposite where Cincinnati now stands. They arrived at the place, and successfully commenced their operations. Boone, instead of taking a part in the diurnal and uninterrupted labor of evaporating the water, performed the more congenial duty of hunting to keep the company in provisions, while they labored. In this pursuit he had one day wandered some distance from the bank of the river. Two Indians, armed with muskets,—for they had now generally added these efficient weapons to their tomahawks—came upon him. His first thought was to retreat. But he discovered from their nimbleness, that this was impossible. His second thought was resistance, and he slipped behind a tree to await their coming within rifle shot. He then exposed himself so as to attract their aim. The foremost levelled his musket. Boone, who could dodge the flash, at the pulling of the trigger, dropped behind his tree unhurt. His next object was to cause the fire of the second musket to be thrown away in the same manner. He again exposed a part of his person. The eager Indian instantly fired, and Boone evaded the shot as before. Both the Indians, having thrown away their fire, were eagerly striving, but with trembling hands, to reload. Trepidation and too much haste retarded their object. Boone drew his rifle and one of them fell dead. The two antagonists, now on equal grounds, the one unsheathing his knife, and the other poising his tomahawk, rushed toward the dead body of the fallen Indian. Boone, placing his foot on the dead body, dexterously received the well aimed tomahawk of his powerful enemy on the barrel of his rifle, thus preventing his skull from being cloven by it. In the very attitude of firing the Indian had exposed his body to the knife of Boone, who plunged it in his body to the hilt. This is the achievement commemorated in sculpture over the southern door of the Rotunda in the Capitol at Washington.

This adventure did not deter him from exposing himself in a similar way again. He was once more hunting for the salt makers, when, on the seventh day of February following, he came in view of a body of one hundred and two Indians, evidently on their march to the assault of Boonesborough—that being a particular mark for Indian revenge. They were in want of a prisoner, from whom to obtain intelligence, and Boone was the person of all others, whom they desired. He fled; but among so many warriors, it proved, that some were swifter of foot than himself, and these overtook him and made him prisoner.

By a tedious and circuitous march they brought him back to the Blue Licks, and took their measures with so much caution, as to make twenty-seven of the thirty salt makers prisoners. Boone obtained for them a capitulation, which stipulated, that their lives should be spared, and that they should be kindly treated. The fortunate three, that escaped, had just been sent home with the salt that had been made during their ill-fated expedition.

The Indians were faithful to the stipulations of the capitulation; and treated their prisoners with as much kindness both on their way, and after their arrival at Chillicothe, as their habits and means would admit. The march was rapid and fatiguing, occupying three days of weather unusually cold and inclement.

The captivity of twenty-eight of the select and bravest of the Kentucky settlers, without the hope of liberation or exchange, was a severe blow to the infant settlement. Had the Indians, after this achievement, immediately marched against Boonesborough, so materially diminished in its means of defence, they might either have taken the place by surprise, or, availing themselves of the influence which the possession of these prisoners gave them over the fears and affections of the inmates, might have procured a capitulation of the fort. Following up this plan in progression, the weaker stations would have followed the example of Boonesborough; since it is hardly supposable, that the united influence of fear, example, and the menace of the massacre of so many prisoners would not have procured the surrender of all the rest. But, though on various occasions they manifested the keenest observation, and the acutest quickness of instinctive cunning—though their plans were generally predicated on the soundest reason, they showed in this, and in all cases, a want of the combination of thought, and the abstract and extended views of the whites on such occasions. For a single effort, nothing could be imagined wiser than their views. For a combination made up of a number of elements of calculation, they had no reasoning powers at all.

Owing to this want of capacity for combined operations of thought, and their habitual intoxication of excitement, on the issue of carrying some important enterprise without loss, they hurried home with their prisoners, leaving the voice of lamentation and the sentiment of extreme dejection among the bereaved inmates of Boonesborough.

Throwing all the recorded incidents and circumstances of the life of Boone, during his captivity among them, together, we shall reserve them for another place, and proceed here to record what befell him among the whites.

He resided as a captive among the Indians until the following March. At that time, he, and ten of the persons who were taken with him at the Blue Licks, were conducted by forty Indians to Detroit, where the party arrived on the thirteenth of the month. The ten men were put into the hands of

Governor Hamilton, who, to his infinite credit, treated them with kindness. For each of these they received a moderate ransom. Such was their respect, and even affection for the hunter of Kentucky, and such, perhaps, their estimate of his capability of annoying them, that although Governor Hamilton offered them the large sum of a hundred pounds sterling for his ransom, they utterly refused to part with him. It may easily be imagined, in what a vexatious predicament this circumstance placed him; a circumstance so much the more embarrassing, as he could not express his solicitude for deliverance, without alarming the jealousy and ill feeling of the Indians. Struck with his appearance and development of character, several English gentlemen, generously impressed with a sense of his painful position, offered him a sum of money adequate to the supply of his necessities. Unwilling to accept such favors from the enemies of his country, he refused their kindness, alleging a motive at once conciliating and magnanimous, that it would probably never be in his power to repay them. It will be necessary to contemplate his desolate and forlorn condition, haggard, and without any adequate clothing in that inclement climate, destitute of money or means, and at the same time to realize that these men, who so generously offered him money, were in league with those that were waging war against the United States, fully to appreciate the patriotism and magnanimity of this refusal. It is very probable, too, that these men acted from the interested motive of wishing to bind the hands of this stern border warrior from any further annoyance to them and their red allies, by motives of gratitude and a sense of obligation.

It must have been mortifying to his spirit to leave his captive associates in comfortable habitations and among a civilized people at Detroit, while he, the single white man of the company, was obliged to accompany his red masters through the forest in a long and painful journey of fifteen days, at the close of which he found himself again at Old Chillicothe, as the town was called.

This town was inhabited by the Shawnese, and Boone was placed in a most severe school, in which to learn Indian modes and ceremonies, by being himself the subject of them. On the return of the party that led him to their home, he learned that some superstitious scruple induced them to halt at mid-day when near their village, in order to solemnize their return by entering their town in the evening. A runner was despatched from their halting place to instruct the chief and the village touching the material incidents of their expedition.

Before the expedition made the triumphal entry into their village, they clad their white prisoner in a new dress, of material and fashion like theirs. They proceeded to shave his head and skewer his hair after their own fashion, and then rouged him with a plentiful smearing of vermilion and put into his hand a white staff, gorgeously tasselated with the tails of deer. The war-captain or leader of the expedition gave as many yells as they had taken prisoners and scalps. This operated as effectually as ringing a tocsin, to assemble the whole village round the camp. As soon as the warriors from the village appeared, four young warriors from the camp, the two first carrying each a calumet, approached the prisoner, chanting a song as they went, and taking him by the arm, led him in triumph to the cabin, where he was to remain until the announcement of his doom. The resident in this cabin, by their immemorial usage, had the power of determining his fate, whether to be tortured and burnt at the stake, or adopted into the tribe.

The present occupant of the cabin happened to be a woman, who had lost a son during the war. It is very probable that she was favorably impressed towards him by noting his fine person, and his firm and cheerful visage—circumstances which impress the women of the red people still more strongly than the men. She contemplated him stedfastly for some time, and sympathy and humanity triumphed, and she declared that she adopted him in place of the son she had lost. The two young men, who bore the calumet, instantly unpinioned his hands, treating him with kindness and respect. Food was brought him, and he was informed that he was considered as a son, and she, who had adopted him, as his mother. He was soon made aware, by demonstrations that could not be dissembled or mistaken, that he was actually loved, and trusted, as if he really were, what his adoption purported to make him. In a few days he suffered no other penalty of captivity than inability to return to his family. He was sufficiently instructed in Indian customs to know well, that any discovered purpose or attempt to escape would be punished with instant death.

Strange caprice of inscrutable instincts and results of habit! A circumstance, apparently fortuitous and accidental, placed him in the midst of an Indian family, the female owner of which loved him with the most disinterested tenderness, and lavished upon him all the affectionate sentiments of a mother towards a son. Had the die of his lot been cast otherwise, all the inhabitants of the village would have raised the death song, and each individual would have been as fiercely unfeeling to torment him, as they were now covetous to show him kindness. It is astonishing to see, in their habits of this sort, no interval between friendship and kindness, and the most ingenious and unrelenting barbarity. Placed between two posts, and his arms and feet extended between them, nearly in the form of a person suffering crucifixion, he would have been burnt to death at a slow fire, while men, women, and children would have danced about him, occasionally applying torches and burning splinters to the most exquisitely sensible parts of the frame, prolonging his torture, and exulting in it with the demoniac exhilaration of gratified revenge.

This was the most common fate of prisoners of war at that time. Sometimes they fastened the victim to a single stake, built a fire of green wood about him, and then raising their yell of exultation, marched off into the desert, leaving him to expire unheeded and alone. At other times they killed their prisoners by amputating their limbs joint by joint. Others they destroyed by pouring on them, from time to time, streams of scalding water. At other times they have been seen to hang their victim to a sapling tree by the hands, bending it down until the wretched sufferer has seen himself swinging up and down at the play of the breeze, his feet often within a foot of the ground. In a word, they seem to have exhausted the invention and ingenuity of all time and all countries in the horrid art of inflicting torture.

The mention of a circumstance equally extraordinary in the Indian character, may be recorded here. If the sufferer in these afflictions be an Indian, during the whole of his agony a strange rivalry passes between them which shall outdo each other, they inflicting, and he in enduring these tortures. Not a groan, not a sigh, not a distortion of countenance is allowed to escape him. He smokes, and looks even cheerful. He occasionally chants a strain of his war song. He vaunts his exploits performed in afflicting death and desolation in their villages. He enumerates the names of their relatives and friends that he has slain. He menaces them with the terrible revenge that his friends will inflict by way of retaliation. He even derides their ignorance in the art of tormenting; assures them that he had afflicted much more ingenious torture upon their people; and indicates more excruciating modes of inflicting pain, and more sensitive parts of the frame to which to apply them.

They are exceedingly dexterous in the horrid surgical operation of taking off the scalp—that is, a considerable surface of the hairy integument of the crown of the cranium. Terrible as the operation is, there are not wanting great numbers of cases of persons who have survived, and recovered from it. The scalps of enemies thus taken, even when not paid for, as has been too often the infamous custom of their white auxiliaries, claiming to be civilized, are valued as badges of family honor, and trophies of the bravery of the warrior. On certain days and occasions, young warriors take a new name, constituting a new claim to honor, according to the number of scalps they have taken, or the bravery and exploits of those from whom they were taken. This name they deem a sufficient compensation for every fatigue and danger. Another ludicrous superstition tends to inspire them with the most heroic sentiments. They believe that all the fame, intelligence, and bravery that appertained to the enemy they have slain is transferred to them, and thenceforward becomes their intellectual property. Hence, they are excited with the most earnest appetite to kill warriors of distinguished fame. This article of Indian faith affords an apt illustration of the ordinary influence of envy, which seems to inspire the person whom it torments with the persuasion, that all the merit it can contract from the envied becomes its own, and that the laurels shorn from another's brow will sprout on its own.

He witnessed also their modes of hardening their children to that prodigious power of unshrinking endurance, of which such astonishing effects have just been recorded. This may be fitly termed the

Indian system of gymnastics. The bodies of the children of both sexes are inured to hardships by compelling them to endure prolonged fastings, and to bathe in the coldest water. A child of eight years, fasts half a day; and one of twelve, a whole day without food or drink. The face is blacked during the fast, and is washed immediately before eating. The male face is entirely blacked; that of the female only on the cheeks. The course is discontinued in the case of the male at eighteen, and of the female at fourteen. At eighteen, the boy is instructed by his parents that his education is completed, and that he is old enough to be a man. His face is then blacked for the last time, and he is removed at the distance of some miles from the village, and placed in a temporary cabin. He is there addressed by his parent or guardian to this purport: "My son, it has pleased the Great Spirit that you should live to see this day. We all have noted your conduct since I first blacked your face. They well understand whether you have strictly followed the advice I have given you, and they will conduct themselves towards you according to their knowledge. You must remain here until I, or some of your friends, come for you."

The party then returns, resumes his gun, and seeming to forget the sufferer, goes to his hunting as usual, and the son or ward is left to endure hunger as long as it can be endured, and the party survive. The hunter, meanwhile, has procured the materials for a feast, of which the friends are invited to partake They accompany the father or guardian to the unfortunate starving subject. He then accompanies them home, and is bathed in cold water, and his head shaved after the Indian fashion--all but a small space on the centre of the crown. He is then allowed to take food, which, however, as a consecrated thing, is presented him in a vessel distinct from that used by the rest. After he has eaten, he is presented with a looking-glass, and a bag of vermilion. He is then complimented for the firmness with which he has sustained his fasting, and is told that he is henceforward a *man*, and to be considered as such. The instance is not known of a boy eating or drinking while under this interdict of the blacked face. They are deterred, not only by the strong sentiments of Indian honor, but by a persuasion that the *Great Spirit* would severely punish such disobedience of parental authority.

The most honorable mode of marriage, and that generally pursued by the more distinguished warriors, is to assemble the friends and relatives, and consult with them in regard to the person whom it is expedient to marry. The choice being made, the relations of the young man collect such presents as they deem proper for the occasion, go to the parents of the woman selected, make known the wishes of their friend, deposit their presents, and return without waiting for an answer. The relations of the girl assemble and consult on the subject. If they confirm the choice, they also collect presents, dress her in her best clothes, and take her to the friends of the bridegroom who made the application for the match, when it is understood that the marriage is completed. She herself has still a negative; and if she disapprove the match, the presents from the friends of the young man are returned, and this is considered as a refusal. Many of the more northern nations, as the Dacotas, for example, have a custom, that, when the husband deceases, his widow immediately manifests the deepest mourning, by putting off all her finery, and dresses herself in the coarsest Indian attire, the sackcloth of Indian lamentation. Meanwhile she makes up a respectable sized bundle of her clothes into the form of a kind of doll-man, which represents her husband. With this she sleeps. To this she converses and relates the sorrows of her desolate heart. It would be indecorous for any warrior, while she is in this predicament, to show her any attentions of gallantry. She never puts on any habiliments but those of sadness and disfigurement. The only comfort she is permitted in this desolate state is, that her budgetted husband is permitted, when drams are passing, to be considered as a living one, and she is allowed to cheer her depressed spirits with a double dram, that of her budget-husband and her own. After a full year of this penance with the budget-husband, she is allowed to exchange it for a living one, if she can find him.

When an Indian party forms for private revenge the object is accomplished in the following manner. The Indian who seeks revenge, proposes his project to obtain it to some of his more intimate associates, and requests them to accompany him. When the requisite number is obtained, and the plan arranged it is kept a profound secret from all others, and the proposer of the plan is considered the leader. The party leaves the village secretly, and in the night. When they halt for the night, the eldest encamp in front, and the younger in the rear. The foremen hunt for the party, and perform the duty of spies. The latter cook, make the fires, mend the moccasins, and perform the other drudgery of the expedition.

Every war party has a small budget, called the *war budget*, which contains something belonging to each one of the party, generally representing some animal; for example, the skin of a snake, the tail of a buffalo, the skin of a martin, or the feathers of some extraordinary bird. This budget is considered a sacred deposit, and is carried by some person selected for the purpose, who marches in front, and leads the party against the enemy. When the party halts, the budget is deposited in front, and no person passes it without authority. No one, while such an exhibition is pending, is allowed to lay his pack on a log, converse about women or his home. When they encamp, the heart of whatever beast they have killed on the preceding day is cut into small pieces and burnt. No person is allowed, while it is burning, to step across the fire, but must go round it, and always in the direction of the sun.

When an attack is to be made, the war budget is opened, and each man takes out his budget, or *totem*, and attaches it to that part of his body which has been indicated by tradition from his ancestors. When the attack is commenced, the body of the fighter is painted, generally black, and is almost naked. After the action, each party returns his *totem* to the commander of the party, who carefully wraps them all up, and delivers them to the man who has taken the first prisoner or scalp; and he is entitled to the honor of leading the party home in triumph. The war budget is then hung in front of the door of the person who carried it on the march against the enemy, where it remains suspended thirty or forty days, and some one of the party often sings and dances round it.

One mode of Indian burial seems to have prevailed, not only among the Indians of the lakes and of the Ohio valley, but over all the western country. Some lay the dead body on the surface of the ground, make a crib or pen over it, and cover it with bark. Others lay the body in a grave, covering it first with bark, and then with earth. Others make a coffin out of the cloven section of trees, in the form of plank, and suspend it from the top of a tree. Nothing can be more affecting than to see a young mother hanging the coffin that contains the remains of her beloved child to the pendent branches of the flowering maple, and singing her lament over her love and hope, as it waves in the breeze.

CHAPTER IX

Boone becomes a favorite among the Indians—Anecdotes relating to his captivity—Their mode of tormenting and burning prisoners—Their fortitude under the infliction of torture—Concerted attack on Boonesborough—Boone escapes.

Boone, being now a son in a principal Shawnee family, presents himself in a new light to our observation. We would be glad to be able give a diurnal record of his modes of deportment, and getting along. Unhappily, the records are few and meagre. It will be obvious, that the necessity for a more profound dissimulation of contentment, cheerfulness, and a feeling of loving his home, was stronger than ever. It was a semblance that must be daily and hourly sustained. He would never have acquitted himself successfully, but for a wonderful versatility, which enabled him to enter into the spirit of whatever parts he was called upon to sustain; and a real love for the hunting and pursuits of the Indians, which rendered what was at first assumed, with a little practice, and the influence of habit, easy and natural. He soon became in semblance so thoroughly one of them, and was able in all those points of practice which give them reputation, to conduct himself with so much skill and adroitness, that he gained the entire confidence of the family into which he was adopted, and become as dear to his mother of adoption as her own son.

Trials of Indian strength and skill are among

their most common amusements. Boone was soon challenged to competition in these trials. In these rencounters of loud laughter and boisterous merriment, where all that was done seemed to pass into oblivion as fast as it transpired, Boone had too much tact and keen observation not to perceive that jealousy, envy, and the origin of hatred often lay hid under the apparent recklessness of indifference. He was not sorry that some of the Indians could really beat him in the race, though extremely light of foot; and that in the game of ball, at which they had been practised all their lives, he was decidedly inferior. But there was another sport—that of shooting at a mark—a new custom to the Indians but recently habituated to the use of fire arms; a practice which they had learned from the whites, and they were excessively jealous of reputation of great skill in this exercise, so important in hunting and war. Boone was challenged to shoot with them at a mark. It placed him in a most perplexing dilemma. If he shot his best, he could easily and far excel their most practised marksmen. But he was aware, that to display his superiority would never be forgiven him. On the other hand, to fall far short of them in an exercise which had been hitherto peculiar to the whites, would forfeit their respect. In this predicament, he judiciously allowed himself sometimes to be beaten; and when it became prudent to put forth all his skill, a well dissembled humility and carelessness subdued the mortification and envy of the defeated competitor.

He was often permitted to accompany them in their hunting parties; and here their habits and his circumstances alike invoked him to do his best. They applauded his skill and success as a hunter, with no mixture of envy or ill will. He was particularly fortunate in conciliating the good will of the Shawnee chief. To attain this result, Boone not only often presented him with a share of his game, but adopted the more winning deportment of always affecting to treat his opinions and counsels with deference. The chief, on his part, often took occasion to speak of Boone as a most consummate proficient in hunting, and a warrior of great bravery. Not long after his residence among them, he had occasion to witness their manner of celebrating their victories, by being an eye witness to one which commemorated the successful return of a war party with some scalps.

Within a day's march of the village, the party dispatched a runner with the joyful intelligence of their success, achieved without loss. Every cabin in the village was immediately ordered to be swept perfectly clean, with the religious intention to banish every source of pollution that might mar the ceremony. The women, exceedingly fearful of contributing in any way to this pollution, commenced an inveterate sweeping, gathering up the collected dirt, and carefully placing it in a heap behind the door. There it remained until the medicine man, or priest, who presides over the powow, ordered them to remove it, and at the same time every savage implement and utensil upon which the women had laid their hands during the absence of the expedition.

Next day the party came in sight of the village, painted in alternate compartments of red and black, their heads enveloped in swan's down, and the centre of their crown, surmounted with long white feathers. They advanced, singing their war song, and bearing the scalps on a verdant branch of evergreen.

Arrived at the village, the chief who had led the party advanced before his warriors to his winter cabin, encircling it in an order of march contrary to the course of the sun, singing the war song after a particular mode, sometimes on the ten or and sometimes on the bass key, sometimes in high and shrill, and sometimes in deep and guttural notes. The *waiter*, or servant of the leader, called *Etissu*, placed a couple of blocks of wood near the war-pole, opposite the door of a circular cabin, called the *hot-house*, in the centre of which was the council fire. On these blocks he rested a kind of ark, deemed among their most sacred things. While this was transacting the party were profoundly silent. The chief bade all set down, and then inquired whether his cabin was prepared and every thing unpolluted, according to the custom of their fathers? After the answer, they rose up in concert and began the war-whoop, walking slowly round the war-pole as they sung. All the consecrated things were then carried, with no small show of solemnity, into the hot-house. Here they remained three whole days and nights, in separation from the rest of the people, applying warm ablutions to their bodies, and sprinkling themselves with a decoction of snake root. During a part of the time, the female relations of each of the consecrated company, after having bathed, anointed, and drest themselves in their finest apparel, stood, in two lines opposite the door, and facing each other. This observance they kept up through the night, uttering a peculiar, monotonous song, in a shrill voice for a minute; then intermitting it about ten minutes, and resuming it again. When not singing their silence was profound.

The chief, meanwhile, at intervals of about three hours, came out at the head of his company, raised the war-whoop, and marched round the red war-pole, holding in his right hand the pine or cedar boughs, on which the scalps were attached, waving them backward and forward, and then returned again. To these ceremonies they conformed without the slightest interruption, during the whole three days' purification. To proceed with the whole details of the ceremony to its close, would be tedious. We close it, only adding, that a small twig of the evergreen was fixed upon the roof of each one of their cabins, with a fragment of the scalps attached to it, and this, as it appeared, to appease the ghosts of their dead. When Boone asked them the meaning of all these long and tedious ceremonies, they answered him by a word which literally imports "holy." The leader and his waiter kept apart and continued the purification three days longer, and the ceremony closed.

He observed, that when their war-parties returned from an expedition, and had arrived near their village, they followed their file leader, in what is called *Indian file*, one by one, each a few yards behind the other, to give the procession an appearance of greater length and dignity. If the expedition had been unsuccessful, and they had lost any of their warriors, they returned without ceremony and in noiseless sadness. But if they had been successful, they fired their guns in platoons, yelling, whooping, and insulting their prisoners, if they had made any. Near their town was a large square area, with a war-pole in the centre, expressly prepared for such purposes. To this they fasten their prisoners. They then advance to the house of their leader, remaining without, and standing round his red war-pole, until they determine concerning the fate of their prisoner. If any prisoner should be fortunate enough to break from his pinions, and escape into the house of the chief medicine man, or conductor of the powow, it is an inviolable asylum, and by immemorial usage, the refugee is saved from the fire.

Captives far advanced in life, or such as had been known to have shed the blood of their tribe, were sure to atone for their decrepitude, or past activity in shedding blood, by being burnt to death. They readily know those Indians who have killed many, by the blue marks on their breasts and arms, which indicate the number they have slain. These hieroglyphics are to them as significant as our alphabetical characters. The ink with which these characters are impressed, is a sort of lampblack, prepared from the soot of burning pine, which they catch by causing it to pass through a sort of greased funnel. Having prepared this lampblack, they tattoo it into the skin, by punctures made with thorns or the teeth of fish. The young prisoners, if they seem capable of activity and service, and if they preserve an intrepid and unmoved countenance, are generally spared, unless condemned to death by the party, while undergoing the purification specified above. As soon as their case is so decided, they are tied to the stake, one at a time. A pair of bear-skin moccasins, with the hair outwards, are put on their feet. They are stripped naked to the loins, and are pinioned firmly to the stake.

Their subsequent punishment, in addition to the suffering of slow fire, is left to the women. Such are the influences of their training, that although the female nature, in all races of men, is generally found to be more susceptible of pity than the male, in this case they appear to surpass the men in the fury of their merciless rage, and the industrious ingenuity of their torments. Each is prepared with a bundle of long, dry, reed cane, or other poles, to which are attached splinters of burning pine. As the victim is led to the stake, the women and children begin their sufferings by beating them with switches and clubs; and as they reel and recoil from the blows, these fiendish imps show their gratification by unremitting peals of laughter; too happy, if their tortures ended here, or if the merciful tomahawk brought them to an immediate close.

The signal for a more terrible infliction being given—the arms of the victim are pinioned, and he is disengaged from the pole, and a grapevine passed round his neck, allowing him a circle of about fifteen yards in circumference, in which he can be made to march round his pole. They knead tough clay on his head to secure the cranium from the effects of the blaze, that it may not inflict immediate death. Under the excitement of ineffable and horrid joy, they whip him round the circle, that he may expose each part of his body to the flame, while the other part is fanned by the cool air, that he may thus undergo the literal operation of slow roasting. During this abhorrent process, the children fill the circle in convulsions of laughter; and the women begin to thrust their burning torches into his body, lacerating the quick of the flesh, that the flame may inflict more exquisite anguish. The warrior, in these cases, goaded to fury, sweeps round the extent of his circle, kicking, biting, and stamping with inconceivable fury. The throng of women and children laugh, and fly from the circle, and fresh tormentors fill it again. At other times the humor takes him to show them, that he can bear all this, without a grimace, a spasm, or indication of suffering. In this case, as we have seen, he smokes, derides, menaces, sings, and shows his contempt, by calling them by the most reproachful of all epithets—*old women*. When he falls insensible, they scalp and dismember him, and the remainder of his body is consumed.

We have omitted many of these revolting details, many of the atrocious features of this spectacle, as witnessed by Boone. While we read with indignation and horror, let us not forget that savages have not alone inflicted these detestable cruelties. Let us not forget that the professed followers of Jesus Christ have given examples of a barbarity equally unrelenting and horrible, in the form of religious persecution, and avowedly to glorify God.

During Boone's captivity among the Shawnese, they took prisoner a noted warrior of a western tribe, with which they were then at war. He was condemned to the stake with the usual solemnities. Having endured the preliminary tortures with the most fearless unconcern, he told them, when preparing to commence a new series, with a countenance of scorn, he could teach them how to make an enemy eat fire to some purpose; and begged that they would give him an opportunity, together with a pipe and tobacco. In respectful astonishment, at an unwonted demonstration of invincible endurance, they granted his request. He lighted his pipe, began to smoke, and sat down, all naked as he was, upon the burning torches, which were blazing within his circle. Every muscle of his countenance retained its composure. On viewing this, a noted warrior sprang up, exclaiming, that this was a true warrior; that though his nation was treacherous, and he had caused them many deaths, yet such was their respect for true courage, that if the fire had not already spoiled him, he should be spared. That being now impossible, he promised him the merciful release of the tomahawk. He then held the terrible instrument suspended some moments over his head, during all which time he

was seen neither to change his posture, move a muscle, or his countenance to blench. The tomahawk fell, and the impassable warrior ceased to suffer.

We shall close these details of the Shawnese customs, at the time when Boone was prisoner among them, by giving his account of their ceremonies at making peace. The chief warriors, who arrange the conditions of the peace and subsequent friendship, first mutually eat and smoke together. They then pledge each other in the sacred drink called *Cussena*. The Shawnese then wave large fans of eagles' tails, and conclude with a dance. The stranger warriors, who have come to receive the peace, select half a dozen of their most active young men, surmounting their crowns with swan's feathers, and painting their bodies with white clay. They then place their file leader on the consecrated seat of what imports in their language, the "beloved cabin." Afterwards they commence singing the peace song, with an air of great solemnity. They begin to dance, first in a prone or bowing posture. They then raise themselves erect, look upwards, and wave their eagles' tails towards the sky, first with a slow, and then with a quick and jerky motion. At the same time, they strike their breast with a calabash fastened to a stick about a foot in length, which they hold in their left hand, while they wave the eagles' feathers with the right, and keep time by rattling pebbles in a gourd. These ceremonies of peace-making they consider among their most solemn duties; and to be perfectly accomplished in all the notes and gestures is an indispensable acquirement to a thorough trained warrior.

Boone has related, at different times, many oral details of his private and domestic life, and his modes of getting along in the family, of which he was considered a member. He was perfectly trained to their ways, could prepare their food, and perform any of their common domestic operations with the best of them. He often accompanied them in their hunting excursions, wandering with them over the extent of forest between Chillicothe and lake Erie. These conversations presented curious and most vivid pictures of their interior modes; their tasks of diurnal labor and supply; their long and severe fasts; their gluttonous indulgence, when they had food; and their reckless generosity and hospitality, when they had any thing to bestow to travelling visitants.

To become, during this tedious captivity, perfectly acquainted with their most interior domestic and diurnal manners, was not without interest for a mind constituted like his. To make himself master of their language, and to become familiarly acquainted with their customs, he considered acquisitions of the highest utility in the future operations, in which, notwithstanding his present duress, he hoped yet to be beneficial to his beloved settlement of Kentucky.

Although the indulgence with which he was treated in the family, in which he was adopted, and these acquisitions, uniting interest with utility, tended to beguile the time of his captivity, it cannot be doubted, that his sleeping and waking thoughts were incessantly occupied with the chances of making his escape. An expedition was in contemplation, by the tribe, to the salt licks on the Scioto, to make salt. Boone dissembled indifference whether they took him with them, or left him behind, with so much success, that, to his extreme joy, they determined that he should accompany them. The expedition started on the first day of June, 1778, and was occupied ten days in making salt.

During this expedition, he was frequently sent out to hunt, to furnish provisions for the party; but always under such circumstances, that, much as he had hoped to escape on this expedition, no opportunity occurred, which he thought it prudent to embrace. He returned with the party to Chillicothe, having derived only one advantage from the journey, that of furnishing, by his making no attempt to escape, and by his apparently cheerful return, new motives to convince the Indians, that he was thoroughly domesticated among them, and had voluntarily renounced his own race; a persuasion, which, by taking as much apparent interest as any of them, in all their diurnal movements and plans, he constantly labored to establish.

Soon after his return he attended a warrior-council, at which, in virtue of being a member of one of the principal families, he had a right of usage and prescription, to be present. It was composed of a hundred and fifty of their bravest men, all painted and armed for an expedition, which he found was intended against Boonesborough. It instantly occurred to him, as a most fortunate circumstance, that he had not escaped on the expedition to Scioto. Higher and more imperious motives, than merely personal considerations, now determined him at every risk to make the effort to escape, and prepare, if he might reach it, the station for a vigorous defence, by forewarning it of what was in preparation among the Indians.

The religious ceremonies of the council and preparation for the expedition were as follow. One of the principal wai chiefs announced the intention of a party to commence an expedition against Boonesborough. This he did by beating their drum, and marching with their war standard three times round the council-house. On this the council dissolved, and a sufficient number of warriors supplied themselves with arms, and a quantity of parched corn flour, as a supply of food for the expedition. All who had volunteered to join in it, then adjourned to their "winter house," and drank the war-drink, a decoction of bitter herbs and roots, for three days —preserving in other respects an almost unbroken fast. This is considered to be an act tending to propitiate the Great Spirit to prosper their expedition. During this period of purifying themselves, they were not allowed to sit down, or even lean upon a tree, however fatigued, until after sun-set. If a bear or deer even passed in sight, custom forbade them from killing it for refreshment. The more rigidly punctual they are in the observance of these rights, the more confidently they expect success.

While the young warriors were under this probation, the aged ones, experienced in the usages of their ancestors, watched them most narrowly to see that, from irreligion, or hunger, or recklessness, they did not violate any of the transmitted religious rites, and thus bring the wrath of the Great Spirit upon the expedition. Boone himself, as a person naturally under suspicion of having a swerving of inclination towards the station to be assailed, was obliged to observe the fast with the most rigorous exactness. During the three days' process of purification, he was not once allowed to go out of the medicine or sanctified ground, without a trusty guard. lest hunger or indifference to their laws should tempt him to violate them.

When the fast and purification was complete, they were compelled to set forth, prepared or unprepared, be the weather fair or foul. Accordingly, when the time arrived, they fired their guns, whooped, and danced, and sung—and continued firing their guns before them on the commencement of their route. The leading war-chief marched first, carrying their medicine bag, or budget of holy things. The rest followed in Indian file, at intervals of three or four paces behind each other, now and then chiming the war-whoop in concert.

They advanced in this order until they were out of sight and hearing of the village. As soon as they reached the deep woods, all became as silent as death. This silence they inculcate, that their ears may be quick to catch the least portent of danger.

Every one acquainted with the race, has remarked their intense keenness of vision. Their eyes, for acuteness, and capability of discerning distant objects, resemble those of the eagle or the lynx; and their cat-like tread among the grass and leaves, seems so light as scarcely to shake off the dew drops. Thus they advance on their expedition rapidly and in profound silence, unless some one of the party should relate that he has had an unpropitious dream. When this happens, an immediate arrest is put upon the expedition, and the whole party face about, and return without any sense of shame or mortification. A whole party is thus often arrested by a single person; and their return is applauded by the tribe, as a respectful docility to the divine impulse, as they deem it, from the Great Spirit. These dreams are universally reverenced, as the warnings of the guardian spirits of the tribe. There is in that country a sparrow, of an uncommon species, and not often seen. This bird is called in the Shawnese dialect by a name importing "kind messenger," which they deem always a true omen, whenever it appears, of bad news. They are exceedingly intimidated whenever this bird sings near them; and were it to perch and sing over their war-camp, the whole party would instantly disperse in consternation and dismay.

Every chief has his warrior, Etissu, or waiter, to attend on him and his party. This confidential personage has charge of every thing that is eaten or drank during the expedition. He parcels it out by rules of rigid abstemiousness. Though each warrior carries on his back all his travelling conveniences, and his food among the rest, yet, however keen the appetite sharpened by hunger, however burning the thirst, no one dares relieve his hunger or thirst, until his rations are dispensed to him by the Etissu.

Boone had occasion to have all these rites most painfully impressed on his memory; for he was obliged to conform to them with the rest. One single thought occupied his mind—to seize the right occasion to escape.

It was sometime before it offered. At length a deer came in sight. He had a portion of his unfinished breakfast in his hand. He expressed a desire to pursue the deer. The party consented. As soon as he was out of sight, he instantly turned his course towards Boonesborough. Aware that he should be pursued by enemies as keen on the scent as bloodhounds, he put forth his whole amount of backwoods skill, in doubling in his track, walking in the water, and availing himself of every imaginable expedient to throw them off his trail. His unfinished fragment of his breakfast was his only food, except roots and berries, during this escape for his life, through unknown forests and pathless swamps, and across numerous rivers, spreading in an extent of more than two hundred miles. Every forest sound must have struck his ear, as a harbinger of the approaching Indians.

No spirit but such an one as his, could have sustained the apprehension and fatigue. No mind but one guided by the intuition of instinctive sagacity, could have so enabled him to conceal his trail, and find his way. But he evaded their pursuit. He discovered his way. He found in roots, in barks, and berries, together with what a single shot of his rifle afforded, wherewith to sustain the cravings of nature. Travelling night and day, in an incredible short space of time he was in the arms of his friends at Boonesborough, experiencing a reception, after such a long and hopeless absence, as words would in vain attempt to portray.

CHAPTER X.

Six hundred Indians attack Boonesborough—Boone and Captain Smith go out to treat with the enemy under a flag of truce, and are extricated from a treacherous attempt to detain them as prisoners—Defence of the fort—The Indians defeated—Boone goes to North Carolina to bring back his family.

It will naturally be supposed that foes less wary and intelligent, than those from whom Boone had escaped, after they had abandoned the hope of recapturing him, would calculate to find Boonesborough in readiness for their reception.

Boonesborough, though the most populous and important station in Kentucky, had been left by the abstraction of so many of the select inhabitants in the captivity of the Blue Licks, by the absence of Colonel Clarke in Illinois, and by the actual decay of the pickets, almost defenceless. Not long before the return of Boone, this important post had been put under the care of Major Smith, an active and intelligent officer. He repaired thither, and put the station, with great labor and fatigue, in a competent state of defence. Learning from the return of some of the prisoners, captured at the Blue Licks, the great blow which the Shawnese meditated against this station, he deemed it advisable to anticipate their movements, and to fit out an expedition to meet them on their own ground.—Leaving twenty young men to defend the place, he marched with thirty chosen men towards the Shawnese towns.

At the Blue Licks, a place of evil omen to Kentucky, eleven of the men, anxious for the safety of the families they had left behind, and deeming their force too small for the object contemplated, abandoned the enterprise and retreated to the fort. The remaining nineteen, not discouraged by the desertion of their companions, heroically persevered. They crossed the Ohio to the present site of Cincinnati, on rafts. They then painted their faces, and in other respects assumed the guise and garb of savages, and marched upon the Indian towns.

When arrived within twenty miles of these towns they met the force with which Boone had set out. Discouraged by his escape, the original party had returned, had been rejoined by a considerable reinforcement, the whole amounting to two hundred and fifty men on horse-back, and were again on their march against Boonesborough. Fortunately, Major Smith and his small party discovered this formidable body before they were themselves observed. But instead of endeavoring to make good their retreat from an enemy so superior in numbers, and mounted upon horses, they fired upon them and killed two of their number. An assault so unexpected alarmed the Indians; and without any effort to ascertain the number of their assailants, they commenced a precipitate retreat. If these rash adventurers had stopped here, they might have escaped unmolested. But, flushed with this partial success, they rushed upon the retreating foe, and repeated their fire. The savages, restored to self-possession, halted in their turn, deliberated a moment, and turned upon the assailants. Major Smith, perceiving the imprudence of having thus put the enemy at bay, and the certainty of the destruction of his little force, if the Indians should perceive its weakness, ordered a retreat in time; and being considerably in advance of the foe, succeeded in effecting it without loss. By a rapid march during the night, in the course of the next morning they reached Boonesborough in safety.

Scarcely an hour after the last of their number had entered the fort, a body of six hundred Indians, in three divisions of two hundred each, appeared with standards and much show of warlike array, and took their station opposite the fort. The whole was commanded by a Frenchman named Duquesne. They immediately sent a flag requesting the surrender of the place, in the name of the king of Great Britain. A council was held, and contrary to the opinion of Major Smith, it was decided to pay no attention to the proposal. They repeated their flag of truce, stating that they had letters from the commander at Detroit to Colonel Boone. On this, it was resolved that Colonel Boone and Major Smith should venture out, and hear what they had to propose.

Fifty yards from the fort three chiefs met them with great parade, and conducted them to the spot designated for their reception, and spread a panther's skin for their seat, while two other Indians held branches over their heads to protect them from the fervor of the sun. The chiefs then commenced an address five minutes in length, abounding in friendly assurances, and the avowal of kind sentiments. A part of the advanced warriors grounded their arms, and came forward to shake hands with them.

The letter from Governor Hamilton of Detroit was then produced, and read. It proposed the most favorable terms of surrender, provided the garrison would repair to Detroit. Major Smith assured them that the proposition seemed a kind one; but that it was impossible, in their circumstances, to remove their women and children to Detroit. The reply was that this difficulty should be removed, for that they had brought forty horses with them, expressly prepared for such a contingency.

In a long and apparently amicable interview, during which the Indians smoked with them, and vaunted their abstinence in not having killed the swine and cattle of the settlement, Boone and Smith arose to return to the fort, and make known these proposals, and to deliberate upon their decision. Twenty Indians accompanied their return as far as the limits stipulated between the parties allowed. The negotiators having returned, and satisfied the garrison that the Indians had no cannon, advised to listen to no terms, but to defend the fort to the last extremity. The inmates of the station resolved to follow this counsel.

In a short time the Indians sent in another flag, with a view, as they stated, to ascertain the result of the deliberations of the fort. Word was sent them, that if they wished to settle a treaty, a place of conference must be assigned intermediate between their camp and the fort. The Indians consented to this stipulation, and deputed thirty chiefs to arrange the articles, though such appeared to be their distrust, that they could not be induced to come nearer than eighty yards from the fort. Smith and Boone with four others were deputed to confer with them. After a close conference of two days, an arrangement was agreed upon, which contained a stipulation, that neither party should cross the Ohio, until after the terms had been decided upon by the respective authorities on either side. The wary heads of this negotiation considered these terms of the Indians as mere lures to beguile confidence.

When the treaty was at last ready for signature, an aged chief, who had seemed to regulate all the proceedings, remarked that he must first go to his people, and that he would immediately return, and sign the instrument. He was observed to step aside in conference with some young warriors. On his return the negotiators from the garrison asked the chief why he had brought young men in place of those who had just been assisting at the council? His answer was prompt and ingenious. It was, that he wished to gratify his young warriors, who desired to become acquainted with the ways of the whites. It was then proposed, according to the custom of both races, that the parties should shake hands. As the two chief negotiators, Smith and Boone, arose to depart, they were both seized from behind.

Suspicious of treachery, they had posted twenty-five men in a bastion, with orders to fire upon the council, as soon as they should see any marks of treachery or violence. The instant the negotiators were seized, the whole besieging force fired upon them, and the fire was as promptly returned by the men in the bastion. The powerful savages who had grasped Boone and Smith, attempted to drag them off as prisoners. The one who held Smith was compelled to release his grasp by being shot dead. Colonel Boone was slightly wounded. A second tomahawk, by which his skull would have been cleft asunder, he evaded, and it partially fell on Major Smith; but being in a measure spent, it did not inflict a dangerous wound. The negotiators escaped to the fort without receiving any other injury. The almost providential escape of Boone and Smith can only be accounted for by the confusion into which the Indians were thrown, as soon as these men were seized, and by the prompt fire of the men concealed in the bastion. Added to this, the two Indians who seized them were both shot dead, by marksmen who knew how to kill the Indians, and at the same time spare the whites, in whose grasp they were held.

The firing on both sides now commenced in earnest, and was kept up without intermission from morning dawn until dark. The garrison, at once exasperated and cheered by the meditated treachery of the negotiation and its result, derided the furious Indians, and thanked them for the stratagem of the negotiation, which had given them time to prepare the fort for their reception. Goaded to desperation

FORT AT BOONSBOROUGH.

by these taunts, and by Duquesne, who harangued them to the onset, they often rushed up to the fort, as if they purposed to storm it. Dropping dead under the cool and deliberate aim of the besieged, the remainder of the forlorn hope, raising a yell of fury and despair, fell back. Other infuriated bands took their place; and these scenes were often repeated, invariably with the same success, until both parties were incapable of taking aim on account of the darkness.

They then procured a quantity of combustible matter, set fire to it, and approached under covert of the darkness, so near the palisades as to throw the burning materials into the fort. But the inmates had availed themselves of the two days' consultation, granted them by the treacherous foe, to procure an ample supply of water; and they had the means of extinguishing the burning faggots as they fell.

Finding their efforts to fire the fort ineffectual, they returned again to their arms, and continued to fire upon the station for some days. Taught a lesson of prudence, however, by what had already befallen them, they kept at such a cautious distance, as that their fire took little effect. A project to gain the place, more wisely conceived, and promising better success, was happily discovered by Colonel Boone. The walls of the fort were distant sixty yards from the Kentucky river. The bosom of the current was easily discernible by the people within. Boone discovered in the morning that the stream near the shore was extremely turbid. He immediately divined the cause.

The Indians had commenced a trench at the water level of the river bank, mining upwards towards the station, and intending to reach the interior by a passage under the wall. He took measures to render their project ineffectual, by ordering a trench to be cut inside the fort, across the line of their subterraneous passage. They were probably apprised of the countermine that was digging within, by the quantity of earth thrown over the wall. But, stimulated by the encouragement of their French engineer, they continued to advance their mine towards the wall, until, from the friability of the soil through which it passed, it fell in, and all their labor was lost. With a perseverance that in a good cause would have done them honor, in no wise discouraged by this failure to intermit their exertions, they returned again to their fire arms, and kept up a furious and incessant firing for some days, but producing no more impression upon the station than before.

During the siege, which lasted eight days, they proposed frequent parleys, requesting the surrender of the place, and professing to treat the garrison with the utmost kindness. They were answered, that they must deem the garrison to be still more brutally fools than themselves, to expect that they would place any confidence in the proposals of wretches who had already manifested such base and stupid treachery. They were bidden to fire on, for that their waste of powder and lead gave the garrison little uneasiness, and were assured that they could not hope the surrender of the place, while there was a man left within it. On the morning of the ninth day from the commencement of the siege, after having, as usual, wreaked their disappointed fury upon the cattle and swine, they decamped, and commenced a retreat.

No Indian expedition against the whites had been known to have had such a disastrous issue for them. During the siege, their loss was estimated by the garrison at two hundred killed, beside a great number wounded. The garrison, on the contrary, protected by the palisades, behind which they could fire in safety, and deliberately prostrate every foe that exposed himself near enough to become a mark, lost but two killed, and had six wounded.

After the siege, the people of the fort, to whom lead was a great object, began to collect the balls that the Indians had fired upon them. They gathered in the logs of the fort, beside those that had fallen to the ground, a hundred and twenty-five pounds. The failure of this desperate attempt, with such a powerful force, seems to have discouraged the Indians and their Canadian allies from making any further effort against Boonesborough. In the autumn of this season, Colonel Boone returned to North Carolina to visit his wife and family.

When he was taken at the Blue Licks, with his associates, who had returned, while he was left behind in a long captivity, during which no more news of him transpired than as if he were actually among the dead, the people of the garrison naturally concluded that he had been killed. His wife and family numbered him as among the dead; and often had they shuddered on the bare recurrence of some one to the probability of the tortures he had undergone. Deeply attached to him, and inconsolable, they could no longer endure a residence which so painfully reminded them of their loss. As soon as they had settled their minds to the conviction that their head would return to them no more, they resolved to leave these forests that had been so fatal to them, and return to the banks of the Yadkin, where were all their surviving connections. A family so respectable and dear to the settlement would not be likely to leave without having to overcome many tender and pressing solicitations to remain, and many promises that if they would, their temporal wants should be provided for.

To all this Mrs. Boone could only object, that Kentucky had indeed been to her, as its name imported, a dark and *Bloody Ground*. She had lost her eldest son by the savage fire before they had reached the country. Her daughter had been made a captive, and had experienced a forbearance from the Indians to her inexplicable. She would have been carried away to the savage towns, and there would have been forcibly married to some warrior, but for the perilous attempt, and improbable success of her father in recapturing her. Now the father himself, her affectionate husband, and the heroic defender of the family, had fallen a sacrifice, probably in the endurance of tortures on which the imagination dared not to dwell. Under the influence of griefs like these, next to the unfailing resource of religion, the heart naturally turns to the sympathy and society of those bound to it by the ties of nature and affinity. They returned to their friends in North Carolina.

It was nearly five years since this now desolate family had started in company with the first emigrating party of families, in high hopes and spirits, for Kentucky. We have narrated their disastrous rencounter with the Indians in Powell's valley, and their desponding return to Clinch river. We have seen their subsequent return to Boonesborough, on Kentucky river. Tidings of the party thus far had reached the relatives of Mrs. Boone's family in North Carolina; but no news from the country west of the Alleghanies had subsequently reached them. All was uncertain conjecture, whether they still lived, or had perished by famine, wild beasts, or the Indians.

At the close of the summer of 1778, the settlement on the Yadkin saw a company on pack horses approaching in the direction from the western wilderness. They had often seen parties of emigrants departing in that direction, but it was a novel spectacle to see one return from that quarter. At the head of that company was a blooming youth, scarcely yet arrived at the age of manhood. It was the eldest surviving son of Daniel Boone. Next behind him was a matronly woman, in weeds, and with a countenance of deep dejection. It was Mrs. Boone. Still behind was the daughter who had been a captive with the Indians. The remaining children were too young to feel deeply. The whole group was respectable in appearance, though clad in skins, and the primitive habiliments of the wilderness. It might almost have been mistaken for a funeral procession. It stopped at the house of Mr. Bryan, the father of Mrs. Boone.

The people of the settlement were not long in collecting to hear news from the west, and learn the fate of their former favorite, Boone, and his family. As Mrs. Boone, in simple and backwood's phrase, related the thrilling story of their adventures, which needed no trick of venal eloquence to convey it to the heart, an abundant tribute of tears from the hearers convinced the bereaved narrator that true sympathy is natural to the human heart. As they shuddered at the dark character of many of the incidents related, it was an hour of triumph, notwithstanding their pity, for those wiser ones, who took care, in an under tone, to whisper that it might be remembered that they had predicted all that had happened.

CHAPTER XI

A sketch of the character and adventures of several other pioneers—Harrod, Kenton, Logan, Ray, McAffee, and others.

Colonel Boone having seen the formidable invasion of Boonesborough successfully repelled, and with such a loss as would not be likely to tempt the Indians to repeat such assaults—and having thus disengaged his mind from public duties, resigned it to the influence of domestic sympathies. The affectionate husband and father, concealing the tenderest heart under a sun-burnt and care-worn visage, was soon seen crossing the Alleghanies in pursuit of his wife and children. The bright star of his morning promise had been long under eclipse; for this journey was one of continued difficulties, vexations, and dangers—so like many of his sufferings already recounted, that we pass them by, fearing the effect of incidents of so much monotony upon the reader's patience. The frame and spirit of the western adventurer were of iron. He surmounted all, and was once more in the bosom of his family on the Yadkin, who, in the language of the Bible, hailed him as one *who had been dead and was alive again; who had been lost and was found.*

Many incidents of moment and interest in the early annals of Kentucky occurred during this reunion of Boone with his family. As his name is forever identified with these annals, we hope it will not be deemed altogether an episode if we introduce here a brief chronicle of those incidents—though not directly associated with the subject of our memoir. In presenting those incidents, we shall be naturally led to speak of some of the other patriarchs of Kentucky—all Boones in their way—all strangely endowed with that peculiar character which fitted them for the time, place, and achievements. We thus discover the foresight of Providence in the arrangement of means to ends. This is no where seen more conspicuously than in the characters of the founders of states and institutions.

During the absence of Colonel Boone, there was a general disposition in Kentucky to retaliate upon the Shawnese some of the injuries and losses which they had so often inflicted upon the infant settlement. Colonel Bowman, with a force of a hundred and sixty men, was selected to command the expedition; and it was destined against Old Chillicothe—the den where the red northern savages had so long concentrated their expeditions against the settlements south of the Ohio.

The force marched in the month of July, 1779, and reached its destination undiscovered by the Indians. A contest commenced with the Indians at early dawn, which lasted until ten in the morning. But, although Colonel Bowman's force sustained itself with great gallantry, the numbers and concealment of the enemy precluded the chance of a victory. He retreated, with an inconsiderable loss, a distance of thirty miles. The Indians, collecting all their forces, pursued and overtook him. Another engagement of two hours ensued, more to the disadvantage of the Kentuckians than the former. Colonel Harrod proposed to mount a number of horse, and make a charge upon the Indians, who continued the fight with great fury. This apparently desperate measure was followed by the happiest results. The Indian front was broken, and their force thrown into irreparable confusion. Colonel Bowman, having sustained a loss of nine killed and one wounded, afterwards continued an unmolested retreat.

In June of the next year, 1780, six hundred Indians and Canadians, commanded by Colonel Bird, a British officer, attacked Riddle's and Martin's stations, at the forks of the Licking, with six pieces of cannon. They conducted this expedition with so much secrecy, that the first intimation of it which the unsuspecting inhabitants had, was being fired upon. Unprepared to resist so formidable a force, provided moreover with cannon, against which their palisade walls would not stand, they were obliged to surrender at discretion. The savages immediately prostrated one man and two women with the tomahawk. All the other prisoners, many of whom were sick, were loaded with baggage and forced to accompany their return march to the Indian towns. Whoever, whether male or female, infant or aged, became unable, from sickness or exhaustion, to proceed, was immediately dispatched with the tomahawk.

The inhabitants, exasperated by the recital of cruelties to the children and women, too horrible to be named, put themselves under the standard of the intrepid and successful General Clarke, who commanded a regiment of United States' troops at the falls of Ohio. He was joined by a number of volunteers from the country, and they marched against Pickaway, one of the principal towns of the Shawnese, on the Great Miami. He conducted this expedition with his accustomed good fortune. He burnt their town to ashes. Beside the dead, which, according to their custom, the Indians carried off, seventeen bodies were left behind. The loss of General Clarke was seventeen killed.

We here present brief outlines of some of the other more prominent western pioneers, the kindred spirits, the Boones of Kentucky. High spirited intelligent, intrepid as they were, they can never supplant the reckless hero of Kentucky and Missouri in our thoughts. It is true, these men deserve to have their memories perpetuated in monumental brass, and the more enduring page of history. But there is a sad interest attached to the memory of Daniel Boone, which can never belong, in an equal degree, to theirs. They foresaw what this beautiful country would become in the hands of its new possessors. Extending their thoughts beyond the ken of a hunter's calculations, they anticipated the consequences of buts and bounds, officers of registry and record, and courts of justice. In due time, they secured a fair and adequate reversion in the soil which they had planted and so nobly defended. Hence, their posterity, with the inheritance of their name and renown, enter into the heritage of their possessions, and find an honorable and an abundant residence in the country which their fathers settled.

Boone, on the contrary, was too simple-minded, too little given to prospective calculations, and his heart in too much what was passing under his eye, to make this thrifty forecast. In age, in penury, landless, and without a home, he is seen leaving Kentucky, then an opulent and flourishing country, for a new wilderness and new scenes of adventure.

Among the names of the conspicuous backwoodsmen who settled the west, we cannot fail to recognize that of James Harrod. He was from the banks of the Monongahela, and among the earliest immigrants to the "Bloody Ground." He descended the Great Kenhawa, and returned to Pennsylvania in 1774. He made himself conspicuous with a party of his friends at the famous contest with the Indians at the "Point." Next year he returned to Kentucky with a party of immigrants, fixing himself at one of the earliest settlements in the country, which, in honor of him, was called Harrodsburgh.

Nature had moulded him of a form and temperament to look the formidable red man in the face. He was six feet, muscular, broad chested, of a firm and animated countenance, keen and piercing eyes, and sparing of speech. He gained himself an imperishable name in the annals of Kentucky, under the extreme disadvantage of not knowing how to read or write! Obliging and benevolent to his neighbors, he was brave and active in their defence. A successful, because a persevering and intelligent hunter, he was liberal to profuseness in the distribution of the spoils. Vigilant and unerring with his rifle, it was at one time directed against the abundant game for the sake of his friends rather than himself; and at others, against the enemies of his country. Guided by the inexplicable instinct of forest skill, he could conduct the wanderer in the woods from point to point through the wilderness, as the needle guides the mariner upon the ocean. So endowed, others equally illiterate, and less gifted, naturally, and from instinct, arranged themselves under his banner, and fearlessly followed such a leader.

If it was reported, that a family, recently arrived in the country, and not yet acquainted with the backwood's modes of supply, was in want of food Harrod was seen at the cabin door, offering the body of a deer or buffalo, which he had just killed. The commencing farmer, who had lost his oxen, or plough horse, in the range, and unused to the vocation of hunting them, or fearful of the Indian rifle, felt no hesitancy, from his known character, in applying to Harrod. He would disappear in the woods, and in the exercise of his own wonderful tact, the lost beast was soon seen driving to the door.

But the precincts of a station, or the field of a farm, were too uncongenial a range for such a spirit as his. To breathe the fresh forest air—to range deserts where man was not to be seen—to pursue the wild deer and buffalo—to trap the bear and the wolf, or beside the still pond, or the unexplored stream, to catch otters and beavers—to bring down the wild turkey from the summit of the highest trees; such were the congenial pursuits in which he delighted.

But, in a higher sphere, and in the service of his

country, he united the instinctive tact and dexterity of a huntsman with the bravery of a soldier. No labor was too severe for his hardihood; no enterprise too daring and forlorn for his adventure; no course too intricate and complicated for his judgment, so far as native talent could guide it. As a Colonel of the militia, he conducted expeditions against the Indians with uncommon success. After the country had become populous, and he a husband and a father, in the midst of an affectionate family, possessed of every comfort—such was the effect of temperament, operating upon habit, that he became often silent and thoughtful in the midst of the social circle, and was seen in that frame to wander away into remote forests, and to bury himself amidst the unpeopled knobs, where, in a few weeks, he would reacquire his cheerfulness. In one of these excursions he disappeared, and was seen no more, leaving no trace to determine whether he died a natural death, was slain by wild beasts, or the tomahawk of the savage.

Among the names of many of the first settlers of Harrodsburgh, are those that are found most prominent in the early annals of Kentucky. In the first list of these we find the names of McGary, Harland, McBride, and Chaplain. Among the young settlers, none were more conspicuous for active, daring, and meritorious service, than James Ray. Prompt at his post at the first moment of alarm, brave in the field, fearless and persevering in the pursuit of the enemy, scarcely a battle, skirmish, or expedition took place in which he had not a distinguished part. Equally expert as a woodsman, and skilful and successful as a hunter, he was often employed as a spy. It is recorded of him that he left his garrison, when short of provisions, by night marched to a forest at the distance of six miles, killed a buffalo, and, loaded with the choice parts of the flesh, returned to regale the hungry inhabitants in the morning. He achieved this enterprise, too, when it was well known that the vicinity was thronged with Indians, lurking for an opportunity to kill. These are the positions which try the daring and skill, the usefulness and value of men, furnishing a criterion which cannot be counterfeited between reality and resemblance.

We may perhaps in this place most properly introduce another of the famous partisans in savage warfare, Simon Kenton, alias Butler, who, from humble beginnings, made himself conspicuous by distinguished services and achievements in the first settlements of this country, and ought to be recorded as one of the patriarchs of Kentucky. He was born in Virginia, in 1753. He grew to maturity without being able to read or write; but from his early exploits he seems to have been endowed with feelings which the educated and those born in the upper walks of life, appear to suppose a monopoly reserved for themselves. It is recorded of him, that at the age of nineteen, he had a violent contest with another competitor for the favor of the lady of his love. She refused to make an election between them, and the subject of this notice indignantly exiled himself from his native place. After various peregrinations on the long rivers of the west, he fixed himself in Kentucky, and soon became a distinguished partisan against the savages. In 1774, he joined himself to Lord Dunmore, and was appointed one of his spies. He made various excursions, and performed important services in this employ. He finally selected a place for improvement on the site where Washington now is. Returning one day from hunting, he found one of his companions slain by the Indians, and his body thrown into the fire. He left Washington in consequence, and joined himself to Colonel Clarke in his fortunate and gallant expedition against Vincennes and Kaskaskia. He was sent by that commander with despatches for Kentucky. He passed through the streets of Vincennes, then in possession of the British and Indians, without discovery. Arriving at White river, he and his party made a raft on which to cross with their guns and baggage, driving their horses into the river and compelling them to swim it. A party of Indians was concealed on the opposite bank, who took possession of the horses as they mounted the bank from crossing the river. Butler and his party seeing this, continued to float down the river on their raft without coming to land. They concealed themselves in the bushes until night, when they crossed the river, pursued their journey, and delivered their despatches.

After this, Butler made a journey of discovery to the northern regions of the Ohio country, and was made prisoner by the Indians. They painted him black, as is their custom when a victim is destined for their torture, and informed him that he was to be burned at Chillicothe. Meanwhile, for their own amusement, and as a prelude of his torture, they manacled him hand and foot, and placed him on an unbridled and unbroken horse, and turned the animal loose, driving it off at its utmost speed, with shouts, delighted at witnessing its mode of managing with its living burden. The horse unable to shake off this new and strange encumbrance, made for the thickest covert of the woods and brambles, with the speed of the winds. It is easy to conjecture the position and suffering of the victim. The terrified animal exhausted itself in fruitless efforts to shake off its burden, and worn down and subdued, brought Butler back amidst the yells of the exulting savages to the camp.

Arrived within a mile of Chillicothe, they halted, took Butler from his horse and tied him to a stake, where he remained twenty-four hours in one position. He was taken from the stake to "run the gauntlet." The Indian mode of managing this kind of torture was as follows: The inhabitants of the tribe, old and young, were placed in parallel lines, armed with clubs and switches. The victim was to make his way to the council house through these files, every member of which struggled to beat him as he passed as severely as possible. If he reached the council house alive, he was to be spared. In the lines were nearly six hundred Indians, and Butler had to make his way almost a mile in the endurance of this infernal sport. He was started by a blow; but soon broke through the files, and had almost reached the council house, when a stout warrior knocked him down with a club. He was severely beaten in this position, and taken back again into custody.

It seems incredible that they sometimes adopted their prisoners, and treated them with the utmost lenity and even kindness. At other times, ingenuity was exhausted to invent tortures, and every renewed endurance of the victim seemed to stimulate their vengeance to new discoveries of cruelty. Butler was one of these ill-fated subjects. No way satisfied with what they had done, they marched him from village to village to give all a spectacle of his sufferings. He run the gauntlet thirteen times. He made various attempts to escape; and in one instance would have effected it, had he not been arrested by some savages who were accidentally returning to the village from which he was escaping. It was finally determined to burn him at the Lower Sandusky, but an apparent accident changed his destiny.

In passing to the stake, the procession went by the cabin of Girty, of whom we have already spoken. This renegado white man lived among these Indians, and had just returned from an unsuccessful expedition against the whites on the frontiers of Pennsylvania. The wretch burned with disappointment and revenge, and hearing that there was a white man going to the torture, determined to wreak his vengeance on him. He found the unfortunate Butler, threw him to the ground, and began to beat him. Butler, who instantly recognized in Girty the quondam companion and playmate of youth, at once made himself known to him. This sacramental tie of friendship, on recognition, caused the savage heart of Girty to relent. He raised him up, and promised to save him. He procured the assemblage of a council, and persuaded the savages to relinquish Butler to him. He took the unfortunate man home, fed, and clothed him, and Butler began to recruit from his wounds and torture. But the relenting of the savages was only transient and momentary. After five days they repented of their relaxation in his favor, reclaimed him, and marched him to Lower Sandusky to be burned there, according to their original purpose. By a fortunate coincidence, he there met the Indian agent from Detroit, who, from motives of humanity, exerted his influence with the savages for his release, and took him with him to Detroit. Here he was paroled by the Governor. He escaped; and being endowed, like Daniel Boone, to be at home in the woods, by a march of thirty days through the wilderness, he reached Kentucky.

In 1784, Simon Kenton reoccupied the settlement, near Washington, which he had commenced in 1775. Associated with a number of people, he erected a block-house, and made a station here. This became an important point of covering and defence for the interior country. Immigrants felt more confidence in landing at Limestone. To render this confidence more complete, Kenton and his associates built a block-house at Limestone. Two men, of the name of Tanner, had made a small settlement the year preceding at Blue Lick, and were now making salt there. The route from Limestone to Lexington became one of the most general travel for immigrants, and many stations sprang up upon it. Travellers to the country had hitherto been compelled to sleep under the open canopy, exposed to the rains and dews of the night. But cabins were now so common, that they might generally repose under a roof that sheltered them from the weather, and find a bright fire, plenty of wood, and with the rustic fare, a most cheerful and cordial welcome. The people of these new regions were hospitable from native inclination. They were hospitable from circumstances. None but those who dwell in a wilderness, where the savages roam and the wolves howl, can understand all the pleasant associations connected with the sight of a stranger of the same race. The entertainer felt himself stronger from the presence of his guest. His offered food and fare were the spoils of the chase. He heard news from the old settlements and the great world; and he saw in the accession of every stranger a new guaranty of the security, wealth, and improvement of the infant country where he had chosen his resting place.

Among other worthy associates of Boone, we may mention the family of McAfee. Two brothers, James and Robert, emigrated from the county of Botetourt, Virginia, and settled on Salt river, six miles from Harrodsburgh. Having revisited their parent country, on their return they brought with them William and George McAfee. In 1777, the Indians destroyed the whole of their valuable stock of cattle, while they were absent from Kentucky.

In 1779 they returned, and settled McAfee's station, which was subsequently compelled to take its full share in the sufferings and dangers of Indian hostilities.

Benjamin Logan immigrated to the country in 1775, as a private citizen. But he was a man of too much character to remain unnoted. As his character developed, he was successively appointed a magistrate, elected a member of the legislature and rose, as a military character, to the rank of general. His parents were natives of Ireland, who emigrated, while young, to Pennsylvania, where they married, and soon afterwards removed to Augusta county, Virginia.

Benjamin, their oldest son, was born there; and at the age of fourteen, lost his father. Charged, at this early age, with the care of a widowed mother, and children still younger than himself, neither the circumstances of his family, of the country, or his peculiar condition, allowed him the chances of education. Almost as unlettered as James Harrod, he was a memorable example of a self-formed man. Great natural acuteness, and strong intellectual powers, were, however, adorned by a disposition of uncommon benevolence. Under the eye of an excellent father, he commenced with the rudiments of common instruction, the soundest lessons of Christian piety and morality, which were continued by the guidance and example of an admirable mother, with whom he resided until he was turned of twenty-one.

His father had deceased intestate, and, in virtue of

the laws then in force, the whole extensive inheritance of his father's lands descended to him, to the exclusion of his brothers and sisters. His example ought to be recorded for the benefit of those grasping children in these days, who, dead to all natural affection, and every sentiment but avarice, seize all that the law will grant, whether equity will sanction it or not. Disregarding this claim of primogeniture, he insisted that the whole inheritance should be parceled into equal shares, of which he accepted only his own. But the generous impulses of his noble nature, were not limited to the domestic circle. His heart was warm with the more enlarged sentiments of patriotism. At the age of twenty-one, he accompanied Colonel Beauquette, as a serjeant, in a hostile expedition against the Indians of the north. Having provided for the comfortable settlement of his mother and family on James River, Virginia, he moved to the Holston, where he settled and married.

Having been in the expedition of Lord Dunmore against the Indians, and having thus acquired a taste for forest marches and incident, he determined, in 1775, to try his fortunes in Kentucky, which country had then just become a theme of discussion. He set forth from his mother's family with three slaves, leaving the rest to her. In Powell's valley he met with Boone, Henderson, and other kindred spirits, and pursued his journey towards Kentucky in company with them. He parted from them, before they reached Boonesborough, and selected a spot for himself, afterwards called Logan's fort, or station.

In the winter of 1776, he removed his family from Holston, and in March, arrived with it in Kentucky. It was the same year in which the daughter of Col. Boone, and those of Col. Calloway were made captives. The whole country being in a state of alarm, he endeavored to assemble some of the settlers that were dispersed in the country called the Crab Orchard, to join him at his cabins, and there form a station of sufficient strength to defend itself against Indian assault. But finding them timid and unresolved, he was himself obliged to desert his incipient settlement, and move for safety to Harrodsburgh. Yet, such was his determination not to abandon his selected spot, that he raised a crop of corn there, defenceless and surrounded on all sides by Indian incursion.

In the winter of 1777, and previous to the attack of Harrodsburgh, he found six families ready to share with him the dangers of the selected spot; and he removed his family with them to his cabins, where the settlement immediately united in the important duty of palisading a station.

Before these arrangements were fully completed as the females of the establishment, on the twentieth of May, were milking their cows, sustained by a guard of their husbands and fathers, the whole party was suddenly assailed by a large body of Indians, concealed in a cane-brake. One man was killed, and two wounded, one mortally, the other severely. The remainder reached the interior of the palisades of safety. The number in all was thirty, half of whom were women and children. A circumstance was now discovered, exceedingly trying to such a benevolent spirit as that of Logan. While the Indians were still firing, and the inmates part exulting in their safety, and the others mourning over their dead and wounded, it was perceived, that one of the wounded, by the name of Harrison, was still alive, and exposed every moment to be scalped by the Indians. All this his wife and family could discern from within. It is not difficult to imagine their agonizing condition, and piercing lamentations for the fate of one so dear to them. Logan discovered, on this occasion, the same keen sensibility to tenderness, and insensibility to danger, that characterized his friend Boone in similar predicaments. He endeavored to rally a few of the small number of the male inmates of the place to join him, and rush out, and assist in attempting to bring the wounded man within the palisades. But so obvious was the danger, so forlorn appeared the enterprise, that no one could be found disposed to volunteer his aid, except a single individual by the name of John Martin. When they had reached the gate, the wounded man raised himself partly erect, and made a movement, as if disposed to try to reach the fort himself. On this, Martin desisted from the enterprise, and left Logan to attempt it alone. He rushed forward to the wounded man. He made some efforts to crawl onwards by the aid of Logan; but weakened by the loss of blood, and the agony of his wounds, he fainted, and Logan taking him up in his arms, bore him towards the fort. A shower of bullets was discharged upon them, many of which struck the palisades close to his head, as he brought the wounded man safe within the gate, and deposited him in the care of his family.

The station, at this juncture, was destitute of both powder and ball; and there was no chance of supply nearer than Holston. All intercourse between station and station was cut off. Without ammunition the station could not be defended against the Indians. The question was, how to obviate this pressing emergency, and obtain a supply? Captain Logan selected two trusty companions, left the fort by night, evaded the besieging Indians, reached the woods, and with his companions made his way in safety to Holston, procured the necessary supply of ammunition, packed it under their care on horseback, giving them directions how to proceed. He then left them, and traversing the forests by a shorter route on foot, he reached the fort in safety, in ten days from his departure. The Indians still kept up the siege with unabated perseverance. The hopes of the diminished garrison had given way to despair. The return of Logan inspired them with renewed confidence.

Uniting the best attributes of a woodsman and a soldier to uncommon local acquaintance with the country, his instinctive sagacity prescribed to him, on this journey, the necessity of deserting the beaten path, where, he was aware, he should be intercepted by the savages. Avoiding, from the same calculation, the passage of the Cumberland Gap, he explored a track in which man, or at least the white man, had never trodden before. We may add, it has never been trodden since. Through cane-brakes and tangled thickets, over cliffs and precipices, and pathless mountains, he made his solitary way. Following his directions implicitly, his companions, who carried the ammunition, also reached the fort, and it was saved.

His rencounters with the Indians, and his hair-breadth escapes make no inconsiderable figure in the subsequent annals of Kentucky. The year after the siege of his fort, on a hunting excursion, he discovered an Indian camp, at Big Flat Spring, two miles from his station. Returning immediately he raised a party, with which he attacked the camp, from which the Indians fled with precipitation, without much loss on their part, and none on his. A short time after he was attacked at the same place, by another party of Indians. His arm was broken by their fire, and he was otherwise slightly wounded in the breast. They even seized the mane of his horse, and he escaped them from their extreme eagerness to take him alive.

No sooner were his wounds healed, than we find him in the fore front of the expedition against the Indians. In 1779, he served as a captain in Bowman's campaign. He signalized his bravery in the unfortunate battle that ensued, and was with difficulty compelled to retire, when retreat became necessary. The next year a party travelling from Harrodsburgh towards Logan's fort, were fired upon by the Indians, and two of them mortally wounded. One, however, survived to reach the fort, and give an account of the fate of his wounded companion. Logan immediately raised a small party of young men, and repaired to the aid of the wounded man, who had crawled out of sight of the Indians behind a clump of bushes. He was still alive. Logan took him on his shoulders, occasionally relieved in sustaining the burden by his younger associates, and in this way conveyed him to the fort. On their return from Harrodsburgh, Logan's party were fired upon, and one of the party wounded. The assailants were repelled with loss; and it was Logan's fortune again to be the bearer of the wounded man upon his shoulders for a long distance, exposed, the while, to the fire of the Indians.

His reputation for bravery and hospitality, and the influence of a long train of connections, caused him to be the instrument of bringing out many immigrants to Kentucky. They were of a character to prove an acquisition to the country. Like his friends, Daniel Boone, and James Harrod, his house was open to all the recent immigrants. In the early stages of the settlement of the country, his station, like Boone's and Harrod's, was one of the main pillars of the colony. Feeling the importance of this station, as a point of support to the infant settlements, he took effectual measures to keep up an intercourse with the other stations, particularly those of Boone and Harrod. Dangerous as this intercourse was, Logan generally travelled alone, often by night, and universally with such swiftness of foot, that few could be found able to keep speed with him.

In the year 1780, he received his commission as Colonel, and was soon after a member of the Virginia legislature at Richmond. In the year 1781, the Indians attacked Montgomery's station, consisting of six families, connected by blood with Colonel Logan. The father and brother of Mrs. Logan were killed, and her sister-in-law, with four children, taken prisoners. This disaster occurred about ten miles from Logan's fort. His first object was to rescue the prisoners, and his next to chastise the barbarity of the Indians. He immediately collected a party of his friends, and repaired to the scene of action. He was here joined by the bereaved relatives of Montgomery's family. He commanded a rapid pursuit of the enemy, who were soon overtaken, and briskly attacked. They faced upon their assailants, but were beaten after a severe conflict. William Montgomery killed three Indians, and wounded a fourth. Two women and three children were rescued. The savages murdered the other child to prevent its being re-taken. The other prisoners would have experienced the same fate, had they not fled for their lives into the thickets.

It would be very easy to extend this brief sketch of some of the more conspicuous pioneers of Kentucky. Their heroic and disinterested services, their lavish prodigality of their blood and property, gave them that popularity which is universally felt to be a high and priceless acquisition. Loved, and trusted, and honored as fathers of their country, while they lived, they had the persuasion of such generous minds as theirs, that their names would descend with blessings to their grateful posterity

CHAPTER XII.

Boone's brother killed, and Boone himself narrowly escapes from the Indians—Assault upon Ashton's station—and upon the station near Shelbyville—Attack upon McAffee's station.

We have already spoken of the elder brother of Col. Boone and his second return to the Yadkin. A fondness for the western valleys seems to have been as deeply engraven in his affections, as in the heart of his brother. He subsequently returned once more with his family to Kentucky. In 1780 we find a younger brother of Daniel Boone resident with him. The two brothers set out on the sixth of October of that year, to revisit the blue Licks. It may well strike us as a singular fact, that Colonel Boone should have felt any disposition to revisit a place that was connected with so many former disasters. But, as a place convenient for the manufacture of salt, it was a point of importance to the rapidly growing settlement. They had manufactured as much salt as they could pack, and were returning to Boonesborough, when they were overtaken by a party of Indians. By the first fire Colonel Boone's brother fell dead by his side. Daniel Boone faced the enemy, and aimed at the foremost Indian, who appeared to have been the slayer of his brother. That Indian fell. By this time he discovered a host advancing upon him. Taking the still loaded rifle of his fallen brother, he prostrated another foe, and while flying from his enemy found time to reload his rifle. The bullets of a dozen muskets whistled about his head; but the distance of the foe rendered them harmless. No scalp would have been of so much value to his pursuers as that of the well known Daniel Boone; and they pursued him with the utmost eagerness. His object was so far to outstrip them, as to be able to conceal his trail, and put them to fault in regard to his course. He made for a little hill, behind which was a stream of water. He sprang into the water and waded up its current for some distance, and then emerged and struck off at right angles to his former course. Darting onward at the height of his speed, he hoped that he had distanced them, and thrown them off his trail. To his infinite mortification, he discovered that his foe, either accidentally, or from their natural sagacity, had rendered all his caution fruitless, and were fiercely pursuing him still. His next expedient was that of a swing by the aid of a grape-vine, which had so well served him on a like occasion before. He soon found one convenient for the experiment, and availed himself of it, as before. This hope was also disappointed. His foe still hung with staunch peseverance on his trail. He now perceived by their movements, that they were conducted by a dog, that easily ran in zig-zag directions, when at fault, until it had re-scented his course. The expedient of Boone was the only one that seemed adequate to save him. His gun was reloaded. The dog was in advance of the Indians, still scenting his track. A rifle shot delivered him from his officious pursuer. He soon reached a point convenient for concealing his trail, and while the Indians were hunting for it, gained so much upon them as to be enabled to reach Boonesborough in safety.

At the close of the autumn of 1780, Kentucky, from being one county, was divided into three, named Jefferson, Fayette, and Lincoln. William Pope, Daniel Boone, and Benjamin Logan, were appointed to the important offices of commanding the militia of their respective counties.

During this year Col. Clarke descended the Ohio, with a part of his Virginia regiment, and after entering the Mississippi, at the first bluff on the eastern bank, he landed and built Fort Jefferson. The occupation of this fort, for the time, added the Chickasaws to the number of hostile Indians that the western people had to encounter. It was soon discovered, that it would be advisable to evacuate it, as a mean of restoring peace. It was on their acknowleged territory. It had been erected without their consent. They boasted it, as a proof of their friendship, that they had never invaded Kentucky; and they indignantly resented this violation of their territory. The evacuation of the fort was the terms of a peace which the Chickasaws faithfully observed.

The winter of 1781, was one of unusual length and distress for the young settlement of Kentucky. Many of the immigrants arrived after the close of the hunting season; and beside, were unskilful in the difficult pursuit of supplying themselves with game. The Indians had destroyed most of the corn of the preceding summer, and the number of persons to be supplied had rapidly increased. These circumstances created a temporary famine, which, added to the severity of the season, inflicted much severe suffering upon the settlement. Boone and Harrod were abroad, breasting the keen forest air, and seeking the retreat of the deer and buffalo, now becoming scarce, as the inhabitants multiplied. These indefatigable and intrepid men supplied the hungry immigrants with the flesh of buffaloes and deers; and the hardy settlers, accustomed to privations, and not to over delicacy in their food, contented themselves to live entirely on meat, until, in the ensuing autumn, they once more derived abundance from the fresh and fertile soil.

In May, 1782, a body of savages assaulted Ashton's station, killed one man, and took another prisoner. Captain Ashton, with twenty-five men, pursued and overtook them. An engagement, which lasted two hours, ensued. But the great superiority of the Indians in number, obliged Captain Ashton to retreat. The loss of this intrepid party was severe. Eight were killed, and four mortally wounded—their brave commander being among the number of the slain. Four children were taken captive from Major Hoy's station, in August following. Unwarned by the fate of Captain Ashton's party, Captain Holden, with the inadequate force of seventeen men, pursued the captors, came up with them, and were defeated with the loss of four men killed, and one wounded.

This was one of the most disastrous periods since the settlement of the country. A number of the more recent and feeble stations, were so annoyed by savage hostility as to be broken up. The horses were carried off, and the cattle killed in every direction. Near Lexington, a man at work in his field, was shot dead by a single Indian, who ran upon his foe to scalp him, and was himself shot dead from the fort, and fell on the body of his foe.

During the severity of winter, the fury of Indian incursion was awhile suspended, and the stern and scarred hunters had a respite of a few weeks about their cabin fires. But in March, the hostilities were renewed, and several marauding parties of Indians entered the country from north of the Ohio. Col. William Lyn, and Captains Tipton and Chapman, were killed by small detachments that waylaid them upon the Beargrass. In pursuit of one of these parties, Captain Aquila White, with seventeen men, trailed the Indians to the Falls of the Ohio. Supposing that they had crossed, he embarked his men in canoes to follow them on the other shore. They had just committed themselves to the stream, when they were fired upon from the shore they had left. Nine of the party were killed or wounded. Yet, enfeebled as the remainder were, they relanded, faced the foe, and compelled them to retreat.

In April following, a station settled by Boone's elder brother, near the present site where Shelbyville now stands, became alarmed by the appearance of parties of Indians in its vicinity. The people, in consternation, unadvisedly resolved to remove to Beargrass. The men accordingly set out encumbered with women, children, and baggage. In this defenceless predicament, they were attacked by the Indians near Long Run. They experienced some loss, and a general dispersion from each other in the woods. Colonel Floyd, in great haste, raised twenty-five men, and repaired to the scene of action, intent alike upon administering relief to the sufferers, and chastisement to the enemy. He divided his party, and advanced upon them with caution. But their superior knowledge of the country, enabled the Indians to ambuscade both divisions, and to defeat them with the loss of half his men; a loss poorly compensated by the circumstance, that a still greater number of the savages fell in the engagement. The number of the latter were supposed to be three times that of Colonel Floyd's party. The Colonel narrowly escaped with his life, by the aid of Captain Samuel Wells, who, seeing him on foot, pursued by the enemy, dismounted and gave him his own horse, and as he fled, ran by his side to support him on the saddle, from which he might have fallen through weakness from his wounds.—This act of Captain Wells was the more magnanimous, as Floyd and himself were not friends at the time. Such noble generosity was not thrown away upon Floyd. It produced its natural effect, and these two persons lived and died friends. It is pleasant to record such a mode of quelling animosity.

Early in May, two men, one of whom was Samuel McAfee, left James McAfee's station, to go to a clearing at a short distance. They had advanced about a fourth of a mile, when they were fired upon. The companion of McAfee fell. The latter turned and fled towards the station. He had not gained more than fifteen steps when he met an Indian. Both paused a moment to raise their guns, in order to discharge them. The muzzles almost touched. Both fired at the same moment. The Indian's gun flashed in the pan, and he fell. McAfee continued his retreat; but before he reached the station, its inmates had heard the report of the guns; and James and Robert, brothers of McAfee, had come out to the aid of those attacked. The three brothers met. Robert, notwithstanding the caution he received from his brother, ran along the path to see the dead Indian. The party of Indians to which he had belonged, were upon the watch among the trees, and several of them placed themselves between Robert and the station, to intercept his return. Soon made aware of the danger to which his thoughtlessness had exposed him, he found all his dexterity and knowledge of Indian warfare requisite to ensure his safety. He sprang from behind one tree to another, in the direction of the station, pursued by an Indian until he reached a fence within a hundred yards of it, which he cleared by a leap. The Indian had posted himself behind a tree to take safe aim.—McAfee was now prepared for him. As the Indian put his head out from the cover of his tree, to look for his object, he caught McAfee's ball in his mouth, and fell. McAfee reached the station in safety.

James, though he did not expose himself as his brother had done, was fired upon by five Indians who lay in ambush. He fled to a tree for protection. Immediately after he had gained one, three or four aimed at him from the other side. The balls scattered earth upon him, as they struck around his feet, but he remained unharmed. He had no sooner entered the inclosure of the station in safety, than Indians were seen approaching in all directions. Their accustomed horrid yells preceded a general attack upon the station. Their fire was returned with spirit, the women running balls as fast as they were required. The attack continued two hours, when the Indians withdrew.

The firing had aroused the neighborhood; and soon after the retreat of the Indians, Major McGary appeared with forty men. It was determined to pursue the Indians, as they could not have advanced far. This purpose was immediately carried into execution. The Indians were overtaken and completely routed. The station suffered inconvenience from the loss of their domestic animals, which were all killed by the Indians, previous to their retreat. One white man was killed and another died of his wounds in a few days. This was the last attack upon this station by the Indians, although it remained for some years a frontier post.

We might easily swell these annals to volumes, by entering into details of the attack of Kincheloe's station, and its defence by Colonel Floyd; the exploits of Thomas Randolph; the captivity of Mrs. Bland and Peake; and the long catalogue of recorded narratives of murders, burnings, assaults, heroic defences, escapes, and the various incidents of Indian warfare upon the incipient settlements. While their barbarity and horror chill the blood, they show us what sort of men the first settlers of the country were, and what scenes they had to witness, and what events to meet, before they prepared for us our present peace and abundance. The danger and apprehension of their condition must have been such, that we cannot well imagine how they could proceed to the operations of building and fencing, with sufficient composure and quietness of spirit, to complete the slow and laborious preliminaries of founding such establishments, as they have transmitted to their children. Men they must have been, who could go firmly and cheerfully to the common occupations of agriculture, with their lives in their hands, and under the constant expectation of being greeted from the thickets and cane-brakes with the rifle bullet and the Indian yell. Even the women were heroes, and their are instances in abundance on record, where, in defence of their children and cabins, they conducted with an undaunted energy of attack or defence, which would throw into shade the vaunted bravery in the bulletins of regular battles.

These magnanimous pioneers seem to have had a presentiment that they had a great work to accomplish—laying the foundations of a state in the wilderness—a work from which they were to be deterred, neither by hunger, nor toil, nor danger, nor death. For tenderness and affection, they had hearts of flesh. For the difficulties and dangers of their positions, their bosoms were of iron. **They feared God, and had no other fear.**

CHAPTER XIII.

Disastrous battle near the Blue Licks—General Clarke's expedition against the Miami towns—Massacre of McClure's family—The horrors of Indian assaults throughout the settlements—General Harmar's expedition—Defeat of General St. Clair—Gen. Wayne's victory, and a final peace with the Indians.

HERE, in the order of the annals of the country, would be the place to present the famous attack of Bryant's station, which we have anticipated by an anachronism, and given already, in order to present the reader with a clear view of a *station*, and the peculiar mode of *attack and defence* in these border wars. The attack upon Bryant's station was made by the largest body of Indians that had been seen in Kentucky, the whole force amounting at least to six hundred men. We have seen that they did not decamp until they had suffered a severe loss of their warriors. They departed with so much precipitation as to have left their tents standing, their fires burning, and their meat roasting. They took the road to the lower Blue Licks.

Colonel Todd, of Lexington, despatched immediate intelligence of this attack to Colonel Trigg, near Harrodsburgh, and Colonel Boone, who had now returned with his family from North Carolina to Boonesborough. These men were prompt in collecting volunteers in their vicinity. Scarcely had the Indians disappeared from Bryant's station, before a hundred and sixty-six men were assembled to march in pursuit of nearly triple their number of Indians. Besides Colonels Trigg, Todd, and Boone, Majors McGary and Harland, from the vicinity of Harrodsburgh, had a part in this command: A council was held, in which, after considering the disparity of numbers, it was still determined to pursue the Indians. Such was their impetuosity, that they could not be persuaded to wait for the arrival of Colonel Logan, who was known to be collecting a strong party to join them.

The march was immediately commenced upon their trail. They had not proceeded far before Colonel Boone, experienced in the habits of Indians and the indications of their purposes, announced that he discovered marks that their foe was making demonstrations of willingness to meet them. He observed that they took no pains to conceal their route, but carefully took measures to mislead their pursuers in regard to their number. Their first purpose was indicated by cutting trees on their path—the most palpable of all directions as to their course. The other was equally concealed by a cautious concentration of their camp, and by the files taking particular care to step in the foot prints of their file leaders, so that twenty warriors might be numbered from the foot-marks only as one.

Still no Indians were actually seen, until the party arrived on the southern bank of the Licking, at the point of the Blue Licks. A body of Indians was here discovered, mounting the summit of an opposite hill, moving leisurely, and apparently without hurry or alarm—retiring slowly from sight, as on a common march.

The party halted. The officers assembled, and a general consultation took place, respecting what was to be done. The alternatives were, whether it was best to cross the Licking at the hazard of an engagement with the Indians; or to wait where they were, reconnoiter the country, act on the defensive, and abide the coming up of Colonel Logan with his force.

Colonels Todd and Trigg, little acquainted with the Indians, were desirous to be guided by the judgment of Colonel Boone. His opinion being called for, he gave it with his usual clearness and circumspection. As regarded the number of the enemy, his judgment was, that it should be counted from three to five hundred. From the careless and leisurely manner of the march of the body, they had seen, he was aware, that the main body was near, and that the show of this small party was probably, with a view to draw on the attack, founded upon an entire ignorance of their numbers. With the localities of the country about the Licks, from his former residence there, he was perfectly acquainted. The river forms, by its curves, an irregular ellipsis, embracing the great ridge and buffalo road leading from the Licks. Its longest line of bisection leads towards Limestone, and is terminated by two ravines heading together in a point, and diverging thence in opposite directions to the river. In his view, it was probable that the Indians had formed an ambuscade behind these ravines, in a position as advantageous for them as it would be dangerous to the party, if they continued their march. He advised that the party should divide; the one half march up the Licking on the opposite side, and crossing at the mouth of a small branch, called Elk creek, fall over upon the eastern curve of the ravine; while the other half should take a position favorable for yielding them prompt co-operation in case of an attack. He demonstrated, that in this way the advantage of position might be taken from the enemy, and turned in their favor. He was decided and pressing, that if it was determined to attack a force superior, before the arrival of Colonel Logan, they ought at least to send out spies and explore the country before they marched the main body over the river.

This wise counsel of Colonel Boone was perfectly accordant with the views of Colonels Todd and Trigg, and of most of the persons consulted on the occasion. But while they were deliberating, Major McGary, patriotic, no doubt, in his intentions, but ardent, rash, hot-headed, and indocile to military rule, guided his horse into the edge of the river, raised the war-whoop in Kentucky style, and exclaimed, in a voice of gay confidence, "All those that are not cowards will follow me; I will show them where the Indians are!" Saying this, he spurred his horse into the water. One and another, under the impulse of such an appeal to their courage, dashed in after him. The council was thus broken up by force. A part caught the rash spirit by sympathy. The rest, who were disposed to listen to better counsels, were borne along, and their suggestions drowned in the general clamor. All counsel and command were at an end. And it is thus that many of the most important events of history have been determined.

The whole party crossed the river, keeping straight forward in the beaten buffalo road. Advanced a little, parties flanked out from the main body, as the irregularity and unevenness of the ground would allow. The whole body moved on in reckless precipitation and disorder, over a surface covered with rocks, laid bare by the trampling of buffaloes, and the washing of the rain of ages. Their course led them in front of the high ridge which extends for some distance to the left of the road. They were decoyed on in the direction of one of the ravines of which we have spoken, by the reappearance of the party of Indians they had first seen.

The termination of this ridge sloped off in a declivity covered with a thick forest of oaks. The ravines were thick set on their banks with small timber, or encumbered with burnt wood, and the whole area before them had been stripped bare of all herbage by the buffaloes that had resorted to the Licks. Clumps of soil here and there on the bare rock supported a few trees, which gave the whole of this spot of evil omen a most singular appearance. The advance of the party was headed by McGary, Harland, and McBride. A party of Indians, as Boone had predicted, that had been ambushed in the woods here met them. A warm and bloody action immediately commenced, and the rifles on either side did fatal execution. It was discovered in a moment that the whole line of the ravine concealed Indians, who, to the number of thrice that of their foes, rushed upon them. Colonels Todd and Trigg, whose position had been on the right, by the movement in crossing, were thrown in the rear. They fell in their places, and the rear was turned. Between twenty and thirty of these brave men had already paid the forfeit of their rashness, when a retreat commenced under the edge of the tomahawk, and the whizzing of Indian bullets. When the party first crossed the river all were mounted. Many had dismounted at the commencement of the action. Others engaged on horseback. On the retreat, some were fortunate enough to recover their horses, and fled on horseback. Others retreated on foot. From the point where the engagement commenced to the Licking river was about a mile's distance. A high and rugged cliff environed either shore of the river, which sloped off to a plain near the Licks. The ford was narrow, and the water above and below it deep. Some were overtaken on the way, and fell under the tomahawk. But the greatest slaughter was at the river. Some were slain in crossing, and some on either shore.

A singular spectacle was here presented in the case of a man by the name of Netherland, who had been derided for his timidity. He was mounted on a fleet and powerful horse, the back of which he had never left for a moment. He was one of the first to recross the Licking. Finding himself safe upon the opposite shore, a sentiment of sympathy came upon him as he looked back and took a survey of the scene of murder going on in the river and on its shore. Many had reached the river in a state of faintness and exhaustion, and the Indians were still cutting them down. Inspired with the feeling of a commander, he cried out in a loud and authoritative voice, "Halt! Fire on the Indians. Protect the men in the river." The call was obeyed. Ten or twelve men instantly turned, fired on the enemy, and checked their pursuit for a moment, thus enabling some of the exhausted and wounded fugitives to evade the tomahawk, already uplifted to destroy them. The brave and benevolent Reynolds, whose reply to Girty has been reported, relinquished his own horse to Colonel Robert Patterson, who was infirm from former wounds, and was retreating on foot. He thus enabled that veteran to escape. While thus signalizing his disinterested intrepidity, he fell himself into the hands of the Indians. The party that took him consisted of three. Two whites passed him on their retreat. Two of the Indians pursued, leaving him under the guard of the third. His captor stooped to tie his moccasin, and he sprang away from him and escaped. It is supposed that one-fourth of the men engaged in this action were commissioned officers. The whole number engaged was one hundred and seventy-six. Of these, sixty were slain, and eight made prisoners. Among the most distinguished names of those who fell, were those of Colonels Todd and Trigg,

Majors Harland and Bulger, Captains Gordon and McBride, and a son of Colonel Boone. The loss of the savages has never been ascertained. It could not have equalled that of the assailants, though some supposed it greater. This sanguinary affair took place August 19, 1782.

Colonel Logan, on ariving at Bryant's station, with a force of three hundred men, found the troops had already marched. He made a rapid advance, in hopes to join them before they should have met with the Indians. He came up with the survivors, on their retreat from their ill-fated contest, not far from Bryant's station. He determined to pursue his march to the battle ground to bury the dead, if he could not avenge their fall. He was joined by many friends of the killed and missing, from Lexington and Bryant's station. They reached the battle ground on the 25th. It presented a heart-rending spectacle. Where so lately had arisen the shouts of the robust and intrepid woodsmen, and the sharp yell of the savages, as they closed in the murderous contest, the silence of the wide forest was now unbroken, except by birds of prey, as they screamed and sailed over the carnage. The heat was so excessive, and the bodies were so changed by it and the hideous gashes and mangling of the Indian tomahawk and knife, that friends could no longer recognize their dearest relatives. They performed the sad rights of sepulture as they might, upon the rocky ground.

The Indian forces that had fought at the Blue Licks, in the exultation of victory and revenge, returned homeward with their scalps. Those from the north—and they constituted the greater numbers—returned quietly. The western bands took their route through Jefferson county, in hopes to add more scalps to the number of their trophies. Colonel Floyd led out a force to protect the country. They marched through the region on Salt river, and saw no traces of Indians. They dispersed on their return. The greater number of them reached their station, and laid down, fatigued and exhausted, without any precaution against a foe. The Indians came upon them in this predicament in the night, and killed several women and children. A few escaped under the cover of the darkness. A woman, taken prisoner that night, escaped from her savage captors by throwing herself into the bushes, while they passed on. She wandered about the woods eighteen days, subsisting only on wild fruits, and was then found and carried to Lynn's station. She survived the extreme state of exhaustion in which she was discovered. Another woman, taken with four children, at the same time, was carried to Detroit.

The terrible blow which the savages had struck at the Blue Licks, excited a general and immediate purpose of retaliation through Kentucky. General Clarke was appointed commander-in-chief, and Colonel Logan next under him in command of the expedition, to be raised for that purpose. The forces were to rendezvous at Licking. The last of September, 1782, General Clarke, with one thousand men, marched from the present site of Cincinnati, for the Indian towns on the Miami. They fell in on their route with the camp of Simon Girty, who would have been completely surprised with his Indians, had not a straggling savage espied the advance, and reported it to them just in season to enable them to scatter in every direction. They soon spread the intelligence that an army from Kentucky was marching upon their towns.

As the army approached the towns on their route, they found that the inhabitants had evacuated them, and fled into the woods. All the cabins at Chillicothe, Piqua, and Willis were burned. Some skirmishing took place, however, in which five Indians were killed, and seven made prisoners, without any loss to the Kentuckians, save the wounding of one man, which afterwards proved mortal. One distinguished Indian surrendered himself, and was afterwards inhumanly murdered by one of the troops, to the deep regret and mortification of General Clarke.

In October, 1785, Mr. McClure and family, in company with a number of other families, were assailed on Skegg's creek. Six of the family were killed, and Mrs. McClure, a child, and a number of other persons made prisoners. The attack took place in the night. The circumstances of the capture of Mrs. McClure, furnish an affecting incident illustrating the invincible force of natural tendernesss. She had concealed herself, with her four children, in the brush of a thicket, which, together with the darkness, screened her from observation. Had she chosen to have left her infant behind, she might have escaped. But she grasped it, and held it to her bosom, although aware that its shrieks would betray their covert. The Indians, guided to the spot by its cries, killed the three larger children, and took her and her infant captives. The unfortunate and bereaved mother was obliged to accompany their march on an untamed and unbroken horse.

Intelligence of these massacres and cruelties circulated rapidly. Captain Whitley immediately collected twenty-one men from the adjoining stations, overtook, and killed two of these savages, retook the desolate mother, her babe, and a negro servant, and the scalps of the six persons whom they had killed. Ten days afterwards, another party of immigrants, led by Mr. Moore, were attacked, and nine of their number killed. Captain Whitley pursued the perpetrators of this bloody act, with thirty men. On the sixth day of pursuit through the wilderness, he came up with twenty Indians, clad in the dresses of those whom they had slain. They dismounted and dispersed in the woods, though not until three of them were killed. The pursuers recovered eight scalps, and all the plunder which the Indians had collected at the late massacre.

An expedition of General Clarke, with a thousand men, against the Wabash Indians, failed in consequence of the impatience and discouragement of his men from want of provisions. Colonel Logan was more successful in an expedition against the Shawnese Indians on the Scioto. He surprised one of the towns, and killed a number of the warriors, and took some prisoners.

In October, 1785, the General Government convoked a meeting of all the Lake and Ohio tribes to meet at the mouth of the Great Miami. The Indians met the summons with a moody indifference and neglect, alleging the continued aggressions of the Kentuckians as a reason for refusing to comply with the summons.

The horrors of Indian assault were occasionally felt in every settlement. We select one narrative in detail, to convey an idea of Indian hostility on the one hand, and the manner in which it was met on the other. A family lived on Coope's run, in Bourbon county, consisting of a mother, two sons of a mature age, a widowed daughter, with an infant in her arms, two grown daughters, and a daughter of ten years. The house was a double cabin. The two grown daughters and the smaller girl were in one division, and the remainder of the family in the other. At evening twilight, a knocking was heard at the door of the latter division, asking in good English, and the customary western phrase, "Who keeps house?" As the sons went to open the door, the mother forbade them, affirming that the persons claiming admittance were Indians. The young men sprang to their guns. The Indians, finding themselves refused admittance at that door, made an effort at the opposite one. That door they soon beat open with a rail, and endeavored to take the three girls prisoners. The little girl sprang away, and might have escaped from them in the darkness and the woods. But the forlorn child, under the natural impulse of instinct, ran for the other door and cried for help. The brothers within, it may be supposed, would wish to go forth and protect the feeble and terrified wailer. The mother, taking a broader view of expedience and duty, forbade them. They soon hushed the cries of the distracted child by the merciless tomahawk. While a part of the Indians were engaged in murdering this child, and another in confining one of the grown girls that they had made captive, the third heroically defended herself with a knife, which she was using at a loom at the moment of attack. The intrepidity she put forth was unavailing. She killed one Indian, and was herself killed by another. The Indians, meanwhile, having obtained possession of one half the house, fired it. The persons shut up in the other half had now no other alternative than to be consumed in the flames rapidly spreading towards them, or to go forth and expose themselves to the murderous tomahawks, that had already laid three of the family in their blood. The Indians stationed themselves in the dark angles of the fence, where, by the bright glare of the flames, they could see every thing, and yet remain themselves unseen. Here they could make a sure mark of all that should escape from within. One of the sons took charge of his aged and infirm mother, and the other of his widowed sister and her infant. The brothers emerged from the burning ruins, separated, and endeavored to spring over the fence. The mother was shot dead as her son was piously aiding her over the fence. The other brother was killed as he was gallantly defending his sister. The widowed sister, her infant, and one of the brothers escaped the massacre, and alarmed the settlement. Thirty men, commanded by Colonel Edwards, arrived next day to witness the appalling spectacle presented around the smoking ruins of this cabin. Considerable snow had fallen, and the Indians were obliged to leave a trail, which easily indicated their path. In the evening of that day, they came upon the expiring body of the young woman, apparently murdered but a few moments before their arrival. The Indians had been premonished of their pursuit by the barking of a dog that followed them. They overtook and killed two of the Indians that had staid behind, apparently as voluntary victims to secure the retreat of the rest.

To prevent immigrants from reaching the country, the Indians infested the Ohio river, and concealed themselves in small parties at different points from Pittsburgh to Louisville, where they laid in ambush and fired upon the boats as they passed. They frequently attempted by false signals to decoy the boats ashore, and in several instances succeeded by these artifices in capturing and murdering whole families, and plundering them of their effects. They even armed and manned some of the boats and scows they had taken, and used them as a kind of floating battery, by means of which they killed and captured many persons approaching the settlements.

The last boat which brought immigrants to the

country down the Ohio, that was known to have been attacked by the Indians, was assaulted in the spring of 1791. This circumstance gives it a claim to be mentioned in this place. It was commanded by Captain Hubbel, and brought immigrants from Vermont. The whole number of men, women, and children amounted to twenty persons. These persons had been forewarned by various circumstances that they noted, that hostile Indians were along the shore waiting to attack them. They came up with other boats descending the river, and bound in the same direction with themselves. They endeavored ineffectually to persuade the passengers to join them, that they might descend in the strength of numbers and union. They continued to move down the river alone. The first attempt upon them was a customary Indian stratagem. A person, affecting to be a white man, hailed them, and requested them to lie by, that he might come on board. Finding that the boat's crew were not to be allured to the shore by this artifice, the Indians put off from the shore in three canoes, and attacked the boat. Never was a contest of this sort maintained with more desperate bravery. The Indians attempted to board the boat, and the inmates made use of all arms of annoyance and defence. Captain Hubbel, although he had been severely wounded in two places, and had the cock of his gun shot off by an Indian fire, still continued to discharge his mutilated gun by a fire-brand. After a long and desperate conflict, in which all the passengers capable of defence but four, had been wounded, the Indians paddled off their canoes to attack the boats left behind. They were successful against the first boat they assailed. The boat yielded to them without opposition. They killed the Captain and a boy, and took the women on board prisoners. Making a screen of these unfortunate women, by exposing them to the fire of Captain Hubbel's boat, they returned to the assault. It imposed upon him the painful alternative, either to yield to the Indians, or to fire into their canoes at the hazard of killing the women of their own people. But the intrepid Captain remarked, that if these women escaped their fire, it would probably be to suffer a more terrible death from the savages. He determined to keep up his fire, even on these hard conditions; and the savages were beaten off a second time. In the course of the engagement, the boat, left to itself, had floated with the current near the north shore, where four or five hundred Indians were collected, who poured a shower of balls upon the boat. All the inmates could do, was to avoid exposure as much as possible, and exercise their patience until the boat should float past the Indian fire. One of the inmates of the boat, seeing, as it slowly drifted on, a fine chance for a shot at an Indian, although warned against it, could not resist the temptation of taking his chance. He raised his head to take aim, and was instantly shot dead. When the boat had drifted beyond the reach of the Indian fire, but two of the nine fighting men on board were found unhurt. Two were killed, and two mortally wounded. The noble courage of a boy on board deserves to be recorded. When the boat was now in a place of safety, he requested his friends to extract a ball that had lodged in the skin of his forehead. When this ball had been extracted, he requested them to take out a piece of bone that had been fractured in his elbow by another shot. When asked by his mother why he had not complained or made known his suffering during the engagement, he coolly replied, intimating that there was noise enough without his, that the Captain had ordered the people to make no noise.

All attempts of the General Government to pacify the Indians, having proved ineffectual, an expedition was planned against the hostile tribes northwest of the Ohio. The object was to bring the Indians to a general engagement; or, if that might not be, to destroy their establishments on the waters of the Scioto and the Wabash. General Harmar was appointed to the command of this expedition. Major Hamtranck, with a detachment, was to make a diversion in his favor up the Wabash.

On the 13th of September, 1791, General Harmar marched from Fort Washington, the present site of Cincinnati, with three hundred and twenty regulars, and effected a junction with the militia of Pennsylvania and Kentucky, which had advanced twenty-five miles in front. The whole force amounted to one thousand four hundred and fifty-three men. Col. Hardin, who commanded the Kentucky militia, was detached with six hundred men, chiefly militia, to reconnoiter. On his approach to the Indian settlements, the Indians set fire to their villages and fled. In order, if possible, to overtake them, he was detached with a smaller force, that could be moved more rapidly. It consisted of two hundred and ten men. A small party of Indians met and attacked them; and the greater part of the militia behaved badly,—leaving a few brave men, who would not fly, to their fate. Twenty-three of the party fell, and seven only made their escape and rejoined the army. Notwithstanding this check, the army succeeded so far as to reduce the remaining towns to ashes, and destroy their provisions.

On their return to Fort Washington, Gen. Harmar was desirous of wiping off, in another action, the disgrace which public opinion had impressed upon his arms. He halted eight miles from Chillicothe, and late at night detached Col. Hardin, with orders to find the enemy, and bring them to an engagement. Early in the morning this detachment reached the enemy, and a severe engagement ensued. The savages fought with desperation. Some of the American troops shrunk; but the officers conducted with great gallantry. Most of them fell, bravely discharging their duty. More than fifty regulars and one hundred militia, including the brave officers, Fontaine, Willys, and Frothingham, were slain.

Harmar, in his official account of this affair, claimed the victory, although the Americans seem clearly to have had the worst of it. At his request, he was tried by a court martial, and honorably acquitted. The enemy had suffered so severely, that they allowed him to return unmolested to Fort Washington.

The terrors and the annoyance of Indian hostilities still hung over the western settlements. The call was loud and general from the frontiers, for ample and efficient protection. Congress placed the means in the hands of the executive. Major General Arthur St. Clair was appointed commander-in-chief of the forces to be employed in the meditated expedition. The objects of it were, to destroy the Indian settlements between the Miamies; to expel them from the country; and establish a chain of posts which should prevent their return during the war. This army was late in assembling in the vicinity of Fort Washington. They marched directly towards the chief establishments of the enemy, building and garrisoning in their way the two intermediate forts, Hamilton and Jefferson. After the detachments had been made for these garrisons, the effective force that remained amounted to something less than two thousand men. To open a road for their march, was a slow and tedious business. Small parties of Indians were often seen hovering about their march; and some unimportant skirmishes took place. As the army approached the enemy's country, sixty of the militia deserted in a body. To prevent the influence of such an example, Major Hamtranck was detached with a regiment in pursuit of the deserters. The army now consisting of one thousand four hundred men, continued its march. On the third of November, 1792, it encamped fifteen miles south of the Miami villages. Having been rejoined by Major Hamtranck, General St. Clair proposed to march immediately against them.

Half an hour before sunrise, the militia was attacked by the savages, and fled in the utmost confusion. They burst through the formed line of the regulars into the camp. Great efforts were made by the officers to restore order; but not with the desired success. The Indians pressed upon the heels of the flying militia, and engaged General Butler with great intrepidity. The action became warm and general; and the fire of the assailants, passing round both flanks of the first line, in a few minutes was poured with equal fury upon the rear. The artillerists in the centre were mowed down, and the fire was the more galling, as it was directed by an invisible enemy, crouching on the ground, or concealed behind trees. In this manner they advanced towards the very mouths of the cannon; and fought with the infuriated fierceness with which success always animates savages. Some of the soldiers exhibited military fearlessness, and fought with great bravery. Others were timid and disposed to fly. With a self-devotion which the occasion required, the officers generally exposed themselves to the hottest of the contest, and fell in great numbers, in desperate efforts to restore the battle.

The commanding general, though he had been for some time enfeebled with severe disease, acted with personal bravery, and delivered his orders with judgment and self-possession. A charge was made upon the savages with the bayonet; and they were driven from their covert with some loss, a distance of four hundred yards. But as soon as the charge was suspended, they returned to the attack. General Butler was mortally wounded; the left of the right wing broken, and the artillerists killed almost to a man. The guns were seized and the camp penetrated by the enemy. A desperate charge was headed by Colonel Butler, although he was severely wounded, and the Indians were again driven from the camp, and the artillery recovered. Several charges were repeated with partial success. The enemy only retreated, to return to the charge, flushed with new ardor. The ranks of the troops were broken, and the men pressed together in crowds, and were shot down without resistance. A retreat was all that remained, to save the remnant of the army. Colonel Darke was ordered to charge a body of savages that intercepted their retreat. Major Clark, with his battalion, was directed to cover the rear. These orders were carried into effect, and a most disorderly retreat commenced. A pursuit was kept up four miles, when, fortunately for the surviving Americans, the natural greediness of the savage appetite for plunder, called back the victorious Indians to the camp, to divide the spoils. The routed troops continued their flight to fort Jefferson, throwing away their arms on the road. The wounded were left here, and the army retired upon fort Washington.

In this fatal battle, fell thirty-eight commissioned officers, and five hundred and ninety-three non-commissioned officers and privates. Twenty-one commissioned officers, many of whom afterwards died of their wounds, and two hundred and forty-two non-commissioned officers and privates were wounded.

The savage force, in this fatal engagement, was led by a Mississago chief, who had been trained to war under the British, during the revolution. So superior was his knowledge of tactics, that the Indian chiefs, though extremely jealous of him, yielded the entire command to him; and he arranged and fought the battle with great combination of military skill. Their force amounted to four thousand; and they stated the Americans killed, at six hundred and twenty, and their own at sixty-five; but it was undoubtedly much greater. They took seven pieces of cannon and two hundred oxen, and many horses. The chief, at the close of the battle, bade the Indians forbear the pursuit of the Americans, as he said they had killed enough.

General Scott, with one thousand mounted volunteers from Kentucky, soon after marched against a party of the victors, at St. Clair's fatal field. He found the Indians rioting in their plunder, riding the oxen in the glee of triumph, and acting as if the whole body was intoxicated. General Scott immediately attacked them. The contest was short but decisive. The Indians had two hundred killed on the spot. The cannon and military stores remaining, were retaken, and the savages completely routed. The loss of the Kentuckians was inconsiderable.

The reputation of the government was now committed in the fortunes of the war. Three additional regiments were directed to be raised. On the motion in congress for raising these regiments, there was an animated, and even a bitter debate. It was urged on one hand, that the expense of such a force would involve the necessity of severe taxation; that too much power was thrown into the hands of the president; that the war had been badly managed, and ought to have been entrusted to the militia of the west, under their own officers; and with more force they urged that no success could be of any avail, so long as the British held those posts within our acknowledged limits, from which the savages were supplied with protection, shelter, arms, advice, and instigation to the war.

On the other hand, the justice of the cause, as a war of defence, and not of conquest, was unquestionable. It was proved, that between 1783 and 1790, no less than one thousand five hundred people of Kentucky had been massacred by the savages, or dragged into a horrid captivity; and that the frontiers of Pennsylvania and Virginia had suffered a loss not much less. It was proved that every effort had been made to pacify the savages without effect. They showed that in 1790, when a treaty was proposed to the savages at the Miami, they first refused to treat, and then asked thirty days for deliberation. It was granted. In the interim, they stated that not less than one hundred and twenty persons had been killed and captured, and several prisoners roasted alive; at the term of which horrors, they refused any answer at all to the proposition to treat. Various other remarks were made in defence of the bill. It tried the strength of parties in congress, and was finally carried.

General St. Clair resigned, and Major General Anthony Wayne was appointed to succeed him. This officer commanded the confidence of the western people, who confided in that reckless bravery, which had long before procured him the appellation of "Mad Anthony." There was a powerful party who still affected to consider this war unnecessary, and every impediment was placed in the way of its success, which that party could devise. To prove to them that the government was still disposed to peace, two excellent officers and valuable men, Col. Hardin, and Major Truman, were severally despatched with propositions of peace. They were both murdered by the savages. These unsuccessful attempts at negotiation, and the difficulties and delays naturally incident to the preparation of such a force, together with the attempts that had been made in congress, to render the war unpopular, had worn away so much time that the season for operations for the year had almost elapsed. But as soon as the negotiations had wholly failed, the campaign was opened with as much vigor as the nature of the case would admit. The general was able, however, to do no more this autumn, than to advance into the forest towards the country of the savages, six miles in advance of fort Jefferson. He took possession of the ground on which the fatal defeat of St. Clair had taken place, in 1792. He here erected a fortification, with the appropriate name of Fort Recovery. His principal camp was called Greenville.

In Kentucky, meanwhile, many of the people clamored against these measures, and loudly insisted that the war ought to be carried on by militia, to be commanded by an officer taken from their state. It was believed, too, by the executive, that the British government, by retaining their posts within our limits, and by various other measures, at least countenanced the Indians in their hostilities. That government took a more decisive measure early in the spring. A British detachment from Detroit, advanced near fifty miles south of that place, and fortified themselves on the Miami of the lakes. In one of the numerous skirmishes which took place between the savages and the advance of General Wayne, it was affirmed, that the British were mingled with the Indians.

On the 8th of August, 1794, General Wayne reached the confluence of the Au Glaize, and the Miami of the lakes. The richest and most extensive settlements of the western Indians were at this place. It was distant only about thirty miles from the post on the Miami, which the British had recently occupied. The whole strength of the enemy, amounting to nearly two thousand warriors, was collected in the vicinity of that post. The regulars of General Wayne were not much inferior in numbers. A reinforcement of one thousand one hundred mounted Kentucky militia, commanded by General Scott, gave a decided superiority to the American force. The general was well aware that the enemy were ready to give him battle, and he ardently desired it. But in pursuance of the settled policy of the United States, another effort was made for the attainment of peace, without the shedding of blood. The savages were exhorted by those who were sent to them, no longer to follow the counsels of the bad men at the foot of the Rapids, who urged them on to the war, but had neither the power nor the inclination to protect them; that to listen to the propositions of the government of the United States, would restore them to their homes, and rescue them from famine. To these propositions they returned only an evasive answer.

On the 20th of August, the army of General Wayne marched in columns. A select battalion, under Major Price, moved as a reconnoitering force in front. After marching five miles, he received so heavy a fire from the savages, concealed as usual, that he was compelled to retreat. The savages had chosen their ground with great judgment They had moved into a thick wood, in advance of the British works, and had taken a position behind fallen timber, prostrated by a tornado. This rendered their position almost inaccessible to horse. They were formed in three regular lines, according to Indian custom, very much extended in front. Their first effort was to turn the left flank of the American army.

The American legion was ordered to advance with trailed arms, and rouse the enemy from his covert at the point of the bayonet, and then deliver its fire. The cavalry, led by Captain Campbell, was ordered to advance between the Indians and the river, where the wood permitted them to penetrate, and charge their left flank. General Scott, at the head of the mounted volunteers, was commanded to make a considerable circuit and turn their right. These, and all the complicated orders of General Wayne, were promptly executed. But such was the impetuosity of the charge made by the first line of infantry, so entirely was the enemy broken by it, and so rapid was the pursuit, that only a small part of the second line, and of the mounted volunteers could take any part in the action. In the course of an hour, the savages were driven more than two miles, and within gun-shot of the British fort.

General Wayne remained three days on the field of battle, reducing the houses and corn-fields, above and below the fort, and some of them within pistol shot of it, to ashes. The houses and stores of Col. M'Kee, an English trader, whose great influence among the savages had been uniformly exerted for the continuance of the war, was burned among the rest. Correspondence upon these points took place between General Wayne and Major Campbell, who commanded the British fort. That of General Wayne was sufficiently firm; and it manifested that the latter only avoided hostilities with him, by acquiescing *in* the destruction of British property within the range of his guns.

On the 28th the army returned to Au Glaize, destroying all the villages and corn within fifty miles of the river. In this decisive battle, the American loss, in killed and wounded, amounted to one hundred and seven, including officers. Among those that fell, were Captain Campbell and Lieutenant Towles. The general bestowed great and merited praise, for their bravery and promptitude in this affair, to all his troops.

The hostility of the Indians still continuing, the whole country was laid waste; and forts were erected in the heart of their settlements, to prevent their return. This seasonable victory, and this determined conduct on the part of the United States, rescued them from a general war with all the nations north-west of the Ohio. The Six Nations had manifested resentments, which were only appeased for the moment, by the suspension of a settlement, which Pennsylvania was making at Presqu' Isle, within their alleged limits. The issue of this battle dissipated the clouds at once which had been thickening in that quarter. Its influence was undoubtedly felt far to the south. The Indian inhabitants of Georgia, and still farther to the south had been apparently on the verge of a war, and had been hardly restrained from hostility by the feeble authority of that state.

No incidents of great importance occurred in this quarter, until August 3d, of the next year when a definitive treaty was concluded by General Wayne, with the hostile Indians north-west of the Ohio. By this treaty, the destructive war which had so long desolated that frontier, was ended in a manner acceptable to the United States. An accommodation was also brought about with the southern Indians, notwithstanding the intrigues of their Spanish neighbors. The regions of the Mississippi valley were opened on all sides to immigration, and res[illegible] from the dread of Indian hostilities.

CHAPTER XIV.

Rejoicings on account of the peace—Boone indulges his propensity for hunting—Kentucky increases in population—Some account of their conflicting land titles—Progress of civil improvement destroying the range of the hunter—Litigation of land titles—Boone loses his lands—Removes from Kentucky to the Kanawha—Leaves the Kanawha and goes to Missouri, where he is appointed Commandant.

The peace which followed the defeat of the northern tribes of Indians by General Wayne, was most grateful to the harassed settlers of the west. The news of it was received every where with the most lively joy. Every one had cause of gratulation. The hardy warriors, whose exploits we have recounted, felt that they were relieved from the immense responsibilities which rested upon them as the guardians and protectors of the infant settlements. The new settlers could now clear their wild lands, and cultivate their rich fields in peace—without fearing the ambush and the rifles of a secret foe; and the tenants of the scattered cabins could now sleep in safety, and without the dread of being wakened by the midnight war-whoop of the savage. Those who had been pent up in forts and stations joyfully sallied forth, and settled wherever the soil and local advantages appeared the most inviting.

Colonel Boone, in particular, felt that a firm and resolute perseverance had finally triumphed over every obstacle. That the rich and boundless valleys of the great west—the garden of the earth—and the paradise of hunters, had been won from the dominion of the savage tribes, and opened as an asylum for the oppressed, the enterprising, and the free of every land. He had travelled in every direction through this great valley. He had descended from the Alleghanies into the fertile regions of Tennessee, and traced the courses of the Cumberland and Tennessee rivers. He had wandered with delight through the blooming forests of Kentucky. He had been carried prisoner by the Indians through the wilderness which is now the state of Ohio to the great lakes of the north; he had traced the head waters of the Kentucky, the Wabash, the Miamies, the Scioto, and other great rivers of the west, and had followed their meanderings to their entrance into the Ohio; he had stood upon the shores of this beautiful river, and gazed with admiration, as he pursued its winding and placid course through endless forests to mingle with the Mississippi; he had caught some glimmerings of the future, and saw with the prophetic eye of a patriot, that this great valley must soon become the abode of millions of freemen; and his heart swelled with joy, and warmed with a transport which was natural to a mind so unsophisticated and disinterested as his.

Boone rejoiced in a peace which put an end to his perils and anxieties, and which now gave him full leisure and scope to follow his darling pursuit of hunting. He had first been led to the country by that spirit of the hunter, which in him amounted almost to a passion. This propensity may be said to be natural to man. Even in cities and populous places we find men so fond of this pastime that they ransack the cultivated fields and enclosures of the farmer, for the purpose of killing the little birds and squirrels, which, from their insignificance, have ventured to take up their abode with civilized man. What, then, must have been the feelings of Boone, to find himself in the grand theatre of the hunter—filled with buffaloes, deer, bears, wild turkeys, and other noble game?

The free exercise of this darling passion had been checked and restrained, ever since the first settlement of the country, by the continued wars and hostile incursions of the Indians. The path of the hunter had been ambushed by the wily savage, and he seldom ventured beyond the purlieus of his cabin, or the station where he resided. He was now free to roam in safety through the pathless wilderness—to camp out in security whenever he was overtaken by night; and to pursue the game wherever it was to be found in the greatest abundance.

Civilization had not yet driven the primitive tenants of the forest from their favorite retreats. Most of the country was still in a state of nature—unsettled and unappropriated. Few fences or inclosures impeded the free range of the hunter, and very few buts and bounds warned him of his being about to trespass upon the private property of some neighbor. Herds of buffaloes and deer still fed upon the rich cane-brake and rank vegetation of the boundless woods, and resorted to the numerous Licks for salt and drink.

Boone now improved this golden opportunity of

indulging in his favorite pursuit. He loved tc wander alone, with his unerring rifle upon his shoulder, through the labyrinths of the tangled forests, and to rouse the wild beast from his secret lair. There was to him a charm in these primeval solitudes which suited his peculiar temperament, and he frequently absented himself on these lonely expeditions for days together. He never was known to return without being loaded with the spoils of the chase. The choicest viands and titbits of all the forest-fed animals were constantly to be found upon his table. Not that Boone was an epicure; far from it. He would have been satisfied with a soldier's fare. In common with other pioneers of his time, he knew what it was to live upon roots and herbs for days together. He had suffered hunger and want in all its forms without a murmur or complaint. But when peace allowed him to follow his profession of a hunter, and to exercise that tact and superiority which so much distinguished him, he selected from the abundance and profusion of the game which fell victims to his skill, such parts as were most esteemed. His friends and neighbors were also, at all times, made welcome to a share of whatever he killed. And he continued to live in this primitive simplicity—enjoying the luxury of hunting, and of roving in the woods, and indulging his generous and disinterested disposition towards his neighbors, for several years after the peace.

In the meantime, while Boone had been thus courting solitude, and absorbed by the engrossing excitement of hunting, the restless spirit of immigration, and of civil and physical improvement, had not been idle. After the peace the tide of population poured into the country in a continual stream, and the busy spirit of civilization was every where making inroads into the ancient forests, and encroaching upon the dominions of the hunter.

In order, however, that the reader may more readily comprehend the causes which operated as grievances to Boone, and finally led him to abandon Kentucky, and seek a home in regions more congenial, it will be necessary to allude to the progress made in population, and the civil polity, and incidents attending the settlement of the country.

The state of Kentucky was not surveyed by the government and laid off into sections and townships, as has been the case with all the lands north of the Ohio. But the government of Virginia had issued land warrants, or certificates, entitling the holder to locate wherever he might choose, the number of acres named in the warrant. They also gave to actual settlers certain pre-emption rights to such lands as they might occupy and improve by building a cabin, raising a crop, &c. The holders of these warrants, after selecting the land which they intended to cover with their titles, were required to enter a survey and description of the tracts selected, in the Land office, which had been opened for the purpose, to be recorded there, for the information of others, and to prevent subsequent holders of warrants from locating the same lands. Yet notwithstanding these precautions, such was the careless manner in which these surveys were made, that many illiterate persons, ignorant of the forms of law, and the necessity of precision in the specification and descriptions of the tracts on which they had laid their warrants, made such loose and vague entries in the land office, as to afford no accurate information to subsequent locators, who frequently laid their warrants on the same tracts. It thus happened that the whole or a part of almost every tract was covered with different and conflicting titles—forming what have been aptly called 'shingle titles'—overlaying and lapping upon each other, as shingles do upon the roof of a building. In this way twice the existing acres of land were sold, and the door opened for endless controversy about boundaries and titles. The following copy of an entry may serve as a specimen of the vagueness of the lines, buts, and bounds of their claims, and as accounting for the flood of litigation that ensued.

"George Smith enters nine hundred acres of land on a treasury warrant, lying on the north side of Kentucky river, a mile below a creek; beginning about twenty poles below a lick; and running down the river westwardly, and northwestwardly for quantity."

It will easily be seen that a description, so general and indefinite in its terms, could serve as no guide to others who might wish to avoid entering the same lands. This defect in providing fcr the certainty and safety of land titles, proved a sore evil to the state of Kentucky. As these lands increased in value and importance, controversies arose as to the ownership of almost every tract; and innumerable suits, great strife and excitement, prevailed in every neighborhood, and continued until within a late period, to agitate the whole body of society. The legislature of the state, by acts of limitation and judicious legislation upon the subject, have finally quieted the titles of the actual occupants.

Among others who made these loose and unfortunate entries, was Daniel Boone. Unaccustomed to the forms of law and technical precision, he was guided by his own views of what was proper and requisite, and made such brief and general entries, as were afterwards held not sufficient to identify the land. He had discovered and explored the country when it was all one vast wilderness—unoccupied, and unclaimed. He and a few other hardy pioneers, by almost incredible hardships, dangers, and sacrifices, had won it from the savage foe; and judging from his own single and generous mind, he did not suppose that question would ever be made of his right to occupy such favorite portions as he might select and pay for. He did not think it possible that any one, knowing these circumstances, could be found so greedy or so heartless, as to grudge him the quiet and unmolested enjoyment of what he had so dearly earned. But in this he was sadly mistaken. A set of speculators and interlopers, who, following in the train of civilization and wealth, came to enrich themselves by monopolizing the rich lands which had thus been won for them, and by the aid of legal advisers, following all the nice requisitions of the law, pounced, among others, upon the lands of our old pioneer He was not at first disturbed by these speculating harpies; and game being plenty, he gave himself little uneasiness about the claims and titles to particular spots, so long as he had such vast hunting grounds to roam in—which, however, he had the sorrow to see daily encroached upon by the new settlements of the immigrants.

But the inroads made by the frequent settlements in his accustomed hunting range, were not the only annoyances which disturbed the simple habits and patriarchal views of Boone. Civilization brought along with it all the forms of law, and the complicated organization of society and civil government, the progress of which had kept pace with the increasing population.

As early as 1783, the territory of Kentucky had been laid off into three counties, and was that year, by law, formed into one District, denominated the District of Kentucky. Regular courts of justice were organized—log court-houses and log jails were erected—judges, lawyers, sheriffs, and juries were engaged in the administration of justice—money began to circulate—cattle and flocks multiplied—reading and writing schools were commenced—more wealthy immigrants began to flock to the country, bringing with them cabinet furniture, and many of the luxuries of more civilized life—and merchandize began to be wagoned from Philadelphia across the mountains to fort Pitt, now Pittsburgh, from whence it was conveyed in flat boats to Maysville and Louisville.

In 1785 a convention was convoked at Danville, who adopted a memorial, addressed to the Legislature of Virginia, and another to the people of Kentucky—suggesting the propriety, and reasons for erecting the new country into an independent state. In the discussion of this question parties arose, and that warmth and excitement were elicited, which are inseparable from the free and unrestrained discussion of public measures.

In 1786 the legislature of Virginia enacted the preliminary provisions for the separation of Kentucky, as an independent state, provided that Congress should admit it into the Union. About this time another source of party discord was opened in agitating debates touching the claims of Kentucky and the West to the navigation of the Mississippi. The inhabitants were informed by malcontents in Western Pennsylvania, that the American Secretary of State was making propositions to the Spanish minister, to cede to Spain the exclusive right of navigation of the Mississippi for twenty-five years. This information as might be supposed, created a great sensation. It had been felt from the beginning of the western settlements, that the right to the free navigation of the Mississippi was of vital importance to the whole western country, and the least relinquishment of this right—even for the smallest space of time, would be of dangerous precedent and tendency. Circulars were addressed by the principal settlers to men of influence in the nation. But before any decisive measures could be taken, Virginia interfered, by instructing her representatives in Congress to make strong representations against the ruinous policy of the measure.

In 1787 commenced the first operations of that mighty engine, the press, in the western country. Nothing could have been wider from the anticipations, perhaps from the wishes of Boone, than this progress of things. But in the order of events, the transition of unlettered backwoods emigrants to a people with a police, and all the engines of civilization was uncommonly rapid. There was no other paper within five hundred miles of the one now established by Mr. Bradford, at Lexington. The political heart-burnings and slander that had hitherto been transmitted through oral channels, were now concentrated for circulation in this gazette.

In April, 1792, Kentucky was admitted into the Union as an independent state; improvements were steadily and rapidly progressing, and notwithstanding the hostility of the Indians, the population of the state was regularly increasing until the peace which followed the victory of Gen. Wayne. After which, as has been observed, the tide of emigration poured into the country with unexampled rapidity.

Litigation in regard to land titles now began to increase, and continued until it was carried to a distressing height. Col. Boone had begun to turn his attention to the cultivation of the choice tracts he had entered; and he looked forward with the consoling thought that he had enough to provide for a large and rising family, by securing to each of his children, as they became of age, a fine plantation. But in the vortex of litigation which ensued, he was not permitted to escape. The speculators who had spread their greedy claims over the lands which had been previously located and paid for by Boone, relying upon his imperfect entries, and some legal flaws in his titles, brought their ejectments against him, and dragged him into a court of law. He employed counsel, and from term to term, was compelled to dance attendance at court. Here the old hunter listened to the quibbles—the subtleties, and to him, inexplicable jargon of the lawyers. His suits were finally decided against him, and he was cast out of the possession of all, or nearly all the lands which he had looked upon as being indubitably his own. The indignation of the old pioneer can well be imagined, as he saw himself thus stript, by the quibbles and intricacies of the law, of all the rewards of his exposures, labors, sufferings, and dangers in the first settlement of Kentucky. He became more than ever disgusted with the grasping and avaricious spirit—the heartless intercourse and technical forms of what is called civilized society.

But having expended his indignation in a transient paroxysm, he soon settled back to his customary mental complacency and self-possession; and as he had no longer any pledge of consequence remaining to him in the soil of Kentucky—and as it was, moreover, becoming on all sides subject to the empire of the cultivator's axe and plough, he resolved to leave the country. He had witnessed with regret the dispersion of the band of pioneers, with whom he had hunted and fought, side by side, and like a band of brothers, shared every hardship and every danger; and he sighed for new fields of adventure, and the excitement of a hunter's life.

Influenced by these feelings, he removed from Kentucky to the great Kanahwa; where he settled near Point Pleasant. He had been informed that buffaloes and deer were still to be found in abundance on the unsettled bottoms of this river, and that it was a fine country for trapping. Here he continued to reside several years. But he was disappointed in his expectations of finding game. The vicinity of the settlements above and below this unsettled region, had driven the buffaloes from the country; and though there were plenty of deer, yet he derived but little success from his trapping. He finally commenced raising stock, and began to turn his attention to agriculture.

While thus engaged, he met with some persons who had returned from a tour up the Missouri, who described to him the fine country bordering upon that river. The vast prairies—the herds of buffaloes—the grizzly bears—the beavers and otters; and above all, the ancient and unexplored forests of that unknown region, fired his imagination, and produced at once a resolve to remove there.

Accordingly, gathering up such useful articles of baggage as were of light carriage, among which his trusty rifle was not forgotten, he started with his family, driving his whole stock of cattle along with him, on a pilgrimage to this new land of promise. He passed through Cincinnati on his way thither in 1798. Being enquired of as to what had induced him to leave all the comforts of home, and so rich and flourishing a country as his dear Kentucky, which he had discovered, and might almost call his own, for the wilds of Missouri? "Too much crowded," replied he—"too crowded—I want more elbow room" He proceeded about forty-five miles above St. Louis, and settled in what is now St. Charles county. This country being still in the possession of the French and Spanish, the ancient laws by which these territories were governed were still in force there. Nothing could be more simple than their whole system of administration. They had no constitution, no king, no legislative assemblies, no judges, juries, lawyers, or sheriffs. An officer, called the Commandant, and the priests, exercised all the functions of civil magistrates, and decided the few controversies which arose among these primitive inhabitants, who held and occupied many things in common. They suffered their ponies, their cattle, their swine, and their flocks, to ramble and graze on the same common prairies and pastures—having but few fences or inclosures, and possessing but little of that spirit of speculation, enterprise, and money-making, which has always characterized the Americans.

These simple laws and neighborly customs suited the peculiar habits and temper of Boone. And as his character for honesty, courage, and fidelity followed him there, he was appointed Commandant for the district of St. Charles by the Spanish Commandant. He retained this command, and continued to exercise the duties of his office with credit to himself, and to the satisfaction of all concerned, until the government of the United States went into effect.

CHAPTER XV.

Anecdotes of Colonel Boone, related by Mr. Audubon—A remarkable instance of memory.

As an evidence of the development of backwoods skill, and a vivid picture of Daniel Boone, we give the following from Mr. Audubon:

"Daniel Boone, or as he was usually called in the Western country, Colonel Boone, happened to spend a night under the same roof with me, more than twenty years ago. We had returned from a shooting excursion, in the course of which his extraordinary skill in the management of a rifle had been fully displayed. On retiring to the room appropriated to that remarkable individual and myself for the night, I felt anxious to know more of his exploits and adventures than I did, and accordingly took the liberty of proposing numerous questions to him. The stature and general appearance of this wanderer of the western forests, approached the gigantic. His chest was broad and prominent; his muscular powers displayed themselves in every limb; his countenance gave indication of his great courage, enterprise, and perseverance; and when he spoke, the very motion of his lips brought the impression, that whatever he uttered could not be otherwise than strictly true. I undressed, whilst he merely took off his hunting shirt, and arranged a few folds of blankets on the floor; choosing rather to lie there, as he observed, than on the softest bed. When we had both disposed of ourselves, each after his own fashion, he related to me the following account of his powers of memory, which I lay before you, kind reader, in his own words, hoping that the simplicity of his style may prove interesting to you.

"I was once," said he, "on a hunting expedition on the banks of the Green river, when the lower parts of this (Kentucky,) were still in the hands of nature, and none but the sons of the soil were looked upon as its lawful proprietors. We Virginians had for some time been waging a war of intrusion upon them, and I, amongst the rest, rambled through the woods, in pursuit of their race, as I now would follow the tracks of any ravenous animal. The Indians outwitted me one dark night, and I was as unexpectedly as suddenly made a prisoner by them. The trick had been managed with great skill; for no sooner had I extinguished the fire of my camp, and laid me down to rest, in full security, as I thought, than I felt myself seized by an indistinguishable number of hands, and was immediately pinioned, as if about to be led to the scaffold for execution. To have attempted to be refractory, would have proved useless and dangerous to my life; and I suffered myself to be removed from my camp to theirs, a few miles distant, without uttering even a word of complaint. You are aware, I dare say, that to act in this manner, was the best policy, as you understand that by so doing, I proved to the Indians at once, that I was born and bred as fearless of death as any of themselves.

When we reached the camp, great rejoicings were

exhibited. Two squaws, and a few papooses, appeared particularly delighted at the sight of me, and I was assured, by very unequivocal gestures and words, that, on the morrow, the mortal enemy of the Red-skins would cease to live. I never opened my lips, but was busy contriving some scheme which might enable me to give the rascals the slip before dawn. The women immediately fell a searching about my hunting shirt for whatever they might think valuable, and fortunately for me, soon found my flask, filled with *Monongahela*, (that is, reader, strong whisky.) A terrific grin was exhibited on their murderous countenances, while my heart throbbed with joy at the anticipation of their intoxication. The crew immediately began to beat their bellie- and sing, as they passed the bottle from mouth to mouth. How often did I wish the flask ten times its size, and filled with aquafortis! I observed that the squaws drank more freely than the warriors, and again my spirits were about to be depressed, when the report of a gun was heard at a distance. The Indians all jumped on their feet. The singing and drinking were both brought to a stand; and I saw with inexpressible joy, the men walk off to some distance, and talk to the squaws. I knew that they were consulting about me, and I foresaw, that in a few moments the warriors would go to discover the cause of the gun having been fired so near their camp. I expected the squaws would be left to guard me. Well, sir, it was just so. They returned; the men took up their guns and walked away. The squaws sat down again, and in less than five minutes they had my bottle up to their dirty mouths, gurgling down their throats the remains of the whisky.

"With what pleasure did I see them becoming more and more drunk, until the liquor took such hold of them that it was quite impossible for these women to be of any service. They tumbled down, rolled about, and began to snore; when I, having no other chance of freeing myself from the cords that fastened me, rolled over and over towards the fire, and after a short time burned them asunder. I rose on my feet; stretched my stiffened sinews; snatched up my rifle, and, for once in my life, spared that of Indians. I now recollect how desirous I once or twice felt to lay open the skulls of the wretches with my tomahawk; but when I again thought upon killing beings unprepared and unable to defend themselves, it looked like murder without need, and I gave up the idea.

"But, sir, I felt determined to mark the spot, and walking to a thrifty ash sapling, I cut out of it three large chips, and ran off. I soon reached the river, soon crossed it, and threw myself deep into the cane-brakes, imitating the tracks of an Indian with my feet, so that no chance might be left for those from whom I had escaped to overtake me.

"It is now nearly twenty years since this happened, and more than five since I left the whites' settlements, which I might probably never have visited again, had I not been called on as a witness in a law-suit that was pending in Kentucky, and which, I really believe, would never have been settled, had

I not come forward, and established the beginning of a certain boundary line. This is the story, sir.

"Mr. —— moved from old Virginia into Kentucky, and having a large tract granted to him in the new state, laid claim to a certain parcel of land adjoining Green river, and as chance would have it, he took for one of his corners the very ash tree on which I had made my mark, and finished his survey of some thousands of acres, beginning, as it is expressed in the deed, "at an ash marked by three distinct notches of the tomahawk of a white man."

"The tree had grown much, and the bark had covered the marks; but, some how or other, Mr. —— heard from some one all that I have already said to you, and thinking that I might remember the spot alluded to in the deed, but which was no longer discoverable, wrote for me to come and try at least to find the place on the tree. His letter mentioned, that all my expenses should be paid; and not caring much about once more going back to Kentucky, I started and met Mr. ——. After some conversation, the affair with the Indians came to my recollection. I considered for a while, and began to think that after all, I could find the very spot, as well as the tree, if it was yet standing.

"Mr. —— and I mounted our horses, and off we went to the Green river bottoms. After some difficulties, for you must be aware, sir, that great changes had taken place in these woods, I found at last the spot where I had crossed the river, and waiting for the moon to rise, made for the course in which I thought the ash tree grew. On approaching the place, I felt as if the Indians were there still, and as if I was still a prisoner among them. Mr. —— and I camped near what I conceived the spot, and waited till the return of day.

"At the rising of the sun I was on foot, and after a good deal of musing, thought that an ash tree then in sight must be the very one on which I had made my mark. I felt as if there could be no doubt of it, and mentioned my thougnt to Mr. ——. "Well, Colonel Boone," said he, "if you think so, I hope it may prove true, but we must have some witnesses; do you stay hereabout, and I will go and bring some of the settlers whom I know." I agreed. Mr. —— trotted off, and I, to pass the time, rambled about to see if a deer was still living in the land. But ah! sir, what a wonderful difference thirty years makes in the country! Why, at the time when I was caught by the Indians, you would not have walked out in any direction for more than a mile without shooting a buck or a bear. There were then thousands of buffaloes on the hills in Kentucky; the land looked as if it would never become poor; and to hunt in those days was a pleasure indeed. But when I was left to myself on the banks of Green river, I dare say for the last time in my life, a few *signs* only of deer were to be seen, and as to a deer itself, I saw none.

"Mr. —— returned, accompanied by three gentlemen. They looked upon me as if I had been Washington himself, and walked to the ash tree which I now called my own, as if in quest of a long lost treasure. I took an axe from one of them and cut a few chips off the bark. Still no signs were to be seen. So I cut again, until I thought it time to be cautious, and I scraped and worked away with my butcher knife, until I *did* come to where my tomahawk had left an impression in the wood. We now went regularly to work, and scraped at the tree with care, until three hacks, as plain as any three notches ever were, could be seen. Mr. —— and the other gentlemen were astonished, and, I must allow, I was as much surprised as pleased, myself. I made affidavit of this remarkable occurrence in the presence of these gentlemen. Mr. —— gained his cause. I left Green river, forever, and came to where we now are; and, sir, I wish you a good night."

CHAPTER XVI.

Progress of improvement in Missouri—Old age of Boone—Death of his wife—He goes to reside with his son—His death—His personal appearance and character.

Soon after the purchase of Missouri from the French by our government, the American system of government began to be introduced there. American laws, American courts, and the whole American system of politics and jurisprudence spread over the country, changing, by degrees, the features of civil society; infusing life and vigor into the body politic, and introducing that restless spirit of speculation and improvement which characterise the people of the United States. The tide of emigration once more swept by the dwelling of Daniel Boone, driving off the game and monopolizing the rich hunting grounds. His office of commandant was merged and lost in the new order of things. He saw that it was in vain to contend with fate; that go where he would, American enterprize seemed doomed to follow him, and to thwart all his schemes of backwoods retirement. He found himself once more surrounded by the rapid march of improvement, and he accommodated himself, as well as he might, to a state of things which he could not prevent. He had the satisfaction of seeing his children well settled around him, and he spent his time in hunting and exploring the new country.

Meantime, old age began to creep upon him by

degrees, and he had the mortification to find himself surpassed in his own favorite pursuit. The *sharp shooters*, and younger hunters could scour the forests with fleeter pace, and bring down the bears and buffaloes with surer aim, than his time-worn frame, and impaired vision would allow. Even the French, with their fleets of periogues, ascended the Missouri to points where his stiffened sinews did not permit him to follow. These volatile and babbling hunters, with their little, and to him despicable shot guns, could bring down a turkey, where the rifle bullet, now directed by his dimmed eye, could not reach. It was in vain that the sights were made more conspicuous by shreds of white paper. No vigor of will can repair the irresistible influence of age. And however the heart and juvenile remembrances of Boone might follow these brisk and talkative hunters to the Rocky mountains and the Western sea, the sad consciousness that years were stronger than the subduer of bears and Indians, came over his mind like a cloud.

Other sorrows came also with age. In March, 1813, he had the misfortune to lose his wife. She had been to him a faithful companion—participating the same heroic and generous nature with himself. She had followed him from North Carolina into the far wilderness, without a road or even a trace to guide their way—surrounded at every step by wild beasts and savages, and was one of the first white women in the state of Kentucky. She had united her fate to his. and in all his hardships, perils, and trials, had stood by him, a meek, yet courageous and affectionate friend. She was now taken from him in his old age, and he felt for a time, that he was alone in the world, and that the principal tie to his own existence was sundered.

About this time, too, the British war with its influence upon the savage auxiliaries of Britain, tended even to the remote forests of Missouri, which rendered the wandering life of a hunter extremely dangerous. He was no longer able to make one of the rangers who pursued the Indians. But he sent numerous substitutes in his children and neighbors.

After the death of his wife, he went to reside with his son Major Nathan Boone, and continued to make his home there until his death. After the peace he occupied himself in hunting, trapping, and exploring the country—being absent sometimes two or three months at a time—solacing his aged ear with the music of his young days—the howl of the nocturnal wolf—and the war song of the prowling savages, heard far away from the companionship of man.

When the writer lived in St. Charles, in 1816, Colonel Boone, with the return of peace, had resumed his Kentucky habits. He resided, as has been observed, with his son on the Missouri—surrounded by the plantations of his children and connections—occasionally farming, and still felling the trees for his winter fire into his door yard; and every autumn, retiring to the remote and moon-illumined cities of the beavers, for the trapping of which, age had taken away none of his capabilities. He could still, by the aid of paper on his rifle sights, bring down an occasional turkey; at the salt licks, he still waylaid the deer; and he found and cut down bee-trees as readily as in his morning days. Never was old age more green, or gray hairs more graceful. His high, calm, bold forehead seemed converted by years, into iron. Decay came to him without infirmity, palsy, or pain—and surrounded and cherished by kind friends, he died as he had lived, composed and tranquil. This event took place in the year 1818, and in the eighty-fourth year of his age.

Frequent enquiries, and opposite statements have been made, in regard to the religious tenets of the Kentucky hunter. It is due to truth to state, that Boone, little addicted to books, knew but little of the bible, the best of all. He worshipped, as he often said, the Great Spirit—for the woods were his books and his temple; and the creed of the red men naturally became his. But such were the truth, simplicity, and kindness of his character, there can be but little doubt, had the gospel of the Son of God been proposed to him, in its sublime truth and reasonableness, that he would have added to all his other virtues, the higher name of Christian.

He was five feet ten inches in height, of a very erect, clean limbed, and athletic form—admirably fitted in structure, muscle, temperament, and habit, for the endurance of the labors, changes, and sufferngs he underwent. He had what phrenologists would have considered a model head—with a forehead peculiarly high, noble, and bold—thin and compressed lips—a mild, clear, blue eye—a large and prominent chin, and a general expression of countenance in which fearlessness and courage sat enthroned, and which told the beholder at a glance, what he had been, and was formed to be.

We have only to add, that the bust of Boone, in Washington, the painting of him ordered by the General Assembly of Missouri, and the engravings of him in general, have—his family being judges—very little resemblance. They want the high port and noble daring of his countenance.

Though ungratefully requited by his country, he has left a name identified with the history of Kentucky, and with the founders and benefactors of our great republic. In all future time, and in every portion of the globe; in history, in sculpture, in song, in eloquence—the name of Daniel Boone will be recorded as the patriarch of Backwoods Pioneers.

His name has already been celebrated by more than one poet. He is the hero of a poem called the "MOUNTAIN MUSE," by our amiable countryman, Bryan. He is supposed to be the original from which the inimitable characters of LEATHER STOCKING, HAWKEYE, and the TRAPPER of the PRAIRIES, in Cooper's novels, were drawn; and we will close these memoirs, with the splendid tribute to the patriarch of backwoodsmen, by the prince of modern poets, Lord Byron.

Of all men, saving Sylla, the man-slayer,
Who passes for in life and death most lucky,
Of the great names which in our faces stare,
The General Boone, backwoodsman of Kentucky,

Was happiest among mortals any where,
For killing nothing, but a bear or buck; he
Enjoy'd the lonely, vigorous, harmless days
Of his old age, in wilds of deepest maze.

Crime came not near him; she is not the child
Of solitude; health shrank not from him, for
Her home is in the rarely trodden wild,
Which, if men seek her not, and death be more
Their choice than life, forgive them, as beguil'd
By habit to what their own hearts abhor—
In cities cag'd. The present case in point I
Cite is, Boone liv'd hunting up to ninety:

And what is stranger, left behind a name,
For which men vainly decimate the throng;
Not only famous, but of that good fame,
Without which glory's but a tavern song;
Simple, serene, the antipodes of shame,
Which hate or envy e'er could tinge with wrong;
An active hermit; even in age the child
Of nature, or the Man of Ross run wild.

'Tis true, he shrank from men even of his nation,
When they built up unto his darling trees;
He mov'd some hundred miles off, for a station,
Where there were fewer houses and more ease.
The inconvenience of civilization
Is, that you neither can be pleased, nor please.
But where he met the individual man,
He showed himself as kind as mortal can.

He was not all alone; around him grew
A sylvan tribe of children of the chase,
Whose young unwaken'd world was always new,
Nor sword, nor sorrow, yet had left a trace

On her unwrinkled brow, nor could you view
A frown on nature's, or on human face.
The free-born forest found, and kept them free,
And fresh as is a torrent or a tree.

And tall, and strong, and swift of foot were they,
Beyond the dwarfing city's pale abortions;
Because their thoughts had never been the prey
Of care or gain; the green woods were their portions
No sinking spirits told them they grew gray,
No fashion made them apes of her distortions.
Simple they were; not savage; and their rifles,
Though very true, were not yet used for trifles.

Motion was in their days; rest in their slumbers;
And cheerfulness, the handmaid of their toil;
Nor yet too many, nor too few their numbers;
Corruption could not make their hearts her soil·
The lust, which stings; the splendor which encumbers,
With the free foresters divide no spoil.
Serene, not sullen, were the solitudes
Of this unsighing people of the woods.

THE END.

ESTILL'S DEFEAT.

One of the most remarkable pioneer fights, in the early history of the West, was that between Captain James Estill and seventeen of his associates, and a party of twenty-five Wyandotte Indians. One of the actors in that sanguinary struggle, Rev. Joseph Proctor, of Estill County, Kentucky, died December 2, 1844, in the full enjoyment of his faculties, at the age of ninety.

On the 19th of March, 1782, Indian rafts, without any one on them, were seen floating down the Kentucky River, past Boonesboro'. Col. Logan at once dispatched intelligence of the fact to Capt. Estill, at his station, fifteen miles from Boonesboro', near the present site of Richmond, Kentucky, with a force of fifteen men, who were directed to march from Lincoln County to Estill's assistance, and instructing Capt. Estill, if the Indians had not appeared there, to scour the country with a reconnoitering party, as it could not be known at what point the attack would be made.

Estill lost not a moment in collecting a force to go in search of the savages, not doubting, from his knowledge of the Indian character, that they designed an immediate attack on his or some of the neighboring stations. From his own and the nearest stations he raised twenty-five men. While Estill and his men were on this excursion the Indians suddenly appeared around his station at daybreak, March 20th, killed and scalped Miss Innis, and took Munk, a slave of Captain Estill, captive. The Indians retreated hastily, in consequence of a highly exaggerated account Munk gave them of the strength of the station, and the number of fighting men in it. No sooner had the Indians commenced their retreat, than the women in the fort (the men all being absent, except one on the sick list,) started two boys—the late General Samuel South and Peter Hacket—on the trail of Capt. Estill, to give information of what had occurred at the fort. The boys came up with Estill early on the morning of the 21st. After a short search Estill's party struck the trail of the retreating Indians. It was resolved to commence pursuit at once. Five men of the party, however, who had families in the fort, feeling uneasy, and unwilling to trust their defense to the few who remained there, returned to the fort, leaving Estill's party thirty-five in number. These pressed forward as rapidly as possible, but night coming on they encamped near the Little Mountain, the present site of Mount Sterling.

They started early the next morning, being obliged to leave ten of the men behind, whose horses were too jaded to travel. They soon discovered, by fresh tracks, that the Indians were not far in advance. They then marched in four lines until about one hour before sunset, when they discovered six of the savages feasting from the body of a buffalo they had killed. The men were ordered to dismount. Some of the party fired without orders, and the Indians fled. A Mr. David Cook, who acted as ensign, was in advance of the company, and seeing one Indian halt, raised his gun and fired. At the same moment another Indian crossed on the opposite side, and both were leveled with the same shot. This occurring in view of the whole company, inspired them all with a high degree of confidence. In the meantime, the main body of Indians heard the alarm and returned, and the two hostile parties, exactly matched in point of numbers, having twenty-five on each side, were now face to face. The ground was highly favorable to the Indian mode of warfare; but Captain Estill and his men, without a moment's hesitation, boldly and fearlessly commenced an attack upon them, and the Indians as boldly and fearlessly (for they were picked warriors) engaged in the bloody combat. It is, however, disgraceful to relate, that, at the very onset of the action, Lieut. Miller, of Estill's party, with six men, "ingloriously fled" from the field, thereby placing in jeopardy the whole of their comrades, and causing the death of many brave men. Estill's party now numbered eighteen, and the Indians twenty-five.

The flank becoming thus unprotected, Captain Estill directed Cook, with three of the men, to take Miller's position, and repel the attack in that quarter, to which this base act of cowardice had exposed the whole party. The ensign with his party where taking the place assigned, when one of them discovered an Indian and shot him, and the three retreated to a little eminence, whence they thought greater execution could be effected with less danger to themselves; but Cook continued to advance without noticing the absence of his comrades, until he had discharged his gun with effect, when he at once retreated; but after running some distance to a large tree, for the purpose of shelter in firing, he unfortunately got entangled in the tops of fallen timber, and halting for a moment, received a ball, which struck him just below the shoulder-blade and came out just below his collar bone. In the meantime, on the main battle-field, at the distance of about fifty yards, the fight raged with great fury, lasting one hour and three-quarters. On either side wounds and death were inflicted, neither party advancing or retreating. "Every man to his man, and every man to his tree." Capt. Estill, at this period, was covered with blood from a wound received early in the action; nine of his brave companions lay dead upon the field, and four others were so disabled by their wounds as to be unable to continue the fight. Estill's fighting men were now reduced to four. Among this number was Joseph Proctor.

Capt. Estill, the brave leader of this Spartan band, was now brought into a personal conflict with a powerful and active Wyandotte warrior. The conflict was for a time fierce and desperate, and keenly and anxiously watched by Proctor, with his finger on the trigger of his unerring rifle. Such, however, was the nature of the struggle between these powerful combatants, that Proctor could not shoot without greatly endangering the life of his captain. Estill had had his arm broken the preceding summer in an engagement with the Indians; and, in the conflict on this occasion, that arm gave way, and in an instant his savage foe buried his knife in Estill's breast; but in the very same moment, the brave Proctor sent a ball from his rifle to the Wyandott's heart. The survivors then drew off as by mutual consent. Thus ended this desperate battle. It wanted nothing but the circumstance of numbers to make it one of the most memorable in ancient or modern times. The loss of the Indians in killed and wounded, notwithstanding the disparity of numbers after the shameful desertion of Miller, was even greater than Capt. Estill's.

It was afterward ascertained by prisoners recaptured from the Wyandottes, that seventeen of the Indians were killed and two severely wounded. This fight was on the same day with the disastrous battle of Blue Licks, March 22, 1782.

There is a tradition derived from the Wyandotte towns, after the peace, that but one of the warriors engaged in this battle ever returned to his nation. It is certain that the chief, who led on the Wyandottes with so much desperation, fell in the action. Throughout this bloody engagement the coölness and bravery of Proctor were unsurpassed. But his conduct after the battle has always elicited the warmest commendation. He brought off the battle-field, and most of the way to the station, on his back, his badly wounded friend, the brave Col. William Irvine, so long and favorably known in Kentucky.

THE END.

www.ingramcontent.com/pod-product-compliance
Lightning Source LLC
LaVergne TN
LVHW010251110826
845151LV00004B/1447